2014 Supplement
Constitutional Law

EDITORIAL ADVISORS

Erwin Chemerinsky
Dean and Distinguished Professor of Law
University of California, Irvine, School of Law

Richard A. Epstein
Laurence A. Tisch Professor of Law
New York University School of Law
Peter and Kirsten Bedford Senior Fellow
The Hoover Institution
Senior Lecturer in Law
The University of Chicago

Ronald J. Gilson
Charles J. Meyers Professor of Law and Business
Stanford University
Marc and Eva Stern Professor of Law and Business
Columbia Law School

James E. Krier
Earl Warren DeLano Professor of Law
The University of Michigan Law School

Richard K. Neumann, Jr.
Professor of Law
Maurice A. Deane School of Law at Hofstra University

Robert H. Sitkoff
John L. Gray Professor of Law
Harvard Law School

David Alan Sklansky
Professor of Law
Stanford Law School

2014 Supplement
Constitutional Law
Seventh Edition

Geoffrey R. Stone
Harry Kalven, Jr., Distinguished Service Professor of Law
University of Chicago Law School

Louis Michael Seidman
Carmack Waterhouse Professor of Constitutional Law
Georgetown University Law Center

Cass R. Sunstein
Felix Frankfurter Professor of Law
Harvard Law School

Mark V. Tushnet
William Nelson Cromwell Professor of Law
Harvard Law School

Pamela S. Karlan
Kenneth & Harle Montgomery Professor of Public Interest Law
Stanford Law School

Copyright © 2014 Geoffrey R. Stone; Jessica and Andrew Seidman; Cass R. Sunstein; Mark Tushnet; Pamela Karlan; and Rebecca and Laura Tushnet

Published by Wolters Kluwer Law & Business in New York.

Wolters Kluwer Law & Business serves customers worldwide with CCH, Aspen Publishers, and Kluwer Law International products. (www.wolterskluwerlb.com)

No part of this publication may be reproduced or transmitted in any form or by any means, electronic or mechanical, including photocopy, recording, or utilized by any information storage or retrieval system, without written permission from the publisher. For information about permissions or to request permissions online, visit us at www.wolterskluwerlb.com, or a written request may be faxed to our permissions department at 212-771-0803.

To contact Customer Service, e-mail customer.service@wolterskluwer.com, call 1-800-234-1660, fax 1-800-901-9075, or mail correspondence to:

> Wolters Kluwer Law & Business
> Attn: Order Department
> PO Box 990
> Frederick, MD 21705

Printed in the United States of America.

1 2 3 4 5 6 7 8 9 0

ISBN 978-1-4548-4172-2

Library of Congress Cataloging-in-Publication Data

The First Amendment / Geoffrey R. Stone . . . [et al.]. — 4th ed.
　　p. cm. — (Aspen casebook series)
　Includes index.
　ISBN 978-1-4548-0706-3 (casebook)
1. Freedom of speech — United States. 2. Freedom of the press — United States. 3. Freedom of religion — United States. 4. United States. Constitution. 1st Amendment.
I. Stone, Geoffrey R.
　KF4770.F558 2012
　342.7308'53 — dc23

2011044674

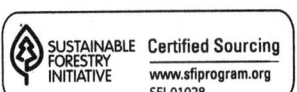

About Wolters Kluwer Law & Business

Wolters Kluwer Law & Business is a leading global provider of intelligent information and digital solutions for legal and business professionals in key specialty areas, and respected educational resources for professors and law students. Wolters Kluwer Law & Business connects legal and business professionals as well as those in the education market with timely, specialized authoritative content and information-enabled solutions to support success through productivity, accuracy and mobility.

Serving customers worldwide, Wolters Kluwer Law & Business products include those under the Aspen Publishers, CCH, Kluwer Law International, Loislaw, ftwilliam.com and MediRegs family of products.

CCH products have been a trusted resource since 1913, and are highly regarded resources for legal, securities, antitrust and trade regulation, government contracting, banking, pension, payroll, employment and labor, and healthcare reimbursement and compliance professionals.

Aspen Publishers products provide essential information to attorneys, business professionals and law students. Written by preeminent authorities, the product line offers analytical and practical information in a range of specialty practice areas from securities law and intellectual property to mergers and acquisitions and pension/benefits. Aspen's trusted legal education resources provide professors and students with high-quality, up-to-date and effective resources for successful instruction and study in all areas of the law.

Kluwer Law International products provide the global business community with reliable international legal information in English. Legal practitioners, corporate counsel and business executives around the world rely on Kluwer Law journals, looseleafs, books, and electronic products for comprehensive information in many areas of international legal practice.

Loislaw is a comprehensive online legal research product providing legal content to law firm practitioners of various specializations. Loislaw provides attorneys with the ability to quickly and efficiently find the necessary legal information they need, when and where they need it, by facilitating access to primary law as well as state-specific law, records, forms and treatises.

ftwilliam.com offers employee benefits professionals the highest quality plan documents (retirement, welfare and non-qualified) and government forms (5500/PBGC, 1099 and IRS) software at highly competitive prices.

MediRegs products provide integrated health care compliance content and software solutions for professionals in healthcare, higher education and life sciences, including professionals in accounting, law and consulting.

Wolters Kluwer Law & Business, a division of Wolters Kluwer, is headquartered in New York. Wolters Kluwer is a market-leading global information services company focused on professionals.

Contents

Table of Cases   *xi*
Table of Authorities   *xiii*

THE SUPREME COURT SINCE 1789   1

I. THE CONSTITUTION AND THE SUPREME COURT   3

F. "Case or Controversy" Requirements and the Passive Virtues   3
    2. Standing   3
        Clapper v. Amnesty International USA   *3*
        Susan B. Anthony List v. Driehaus   *14*

II. FEDERALISM AT WORK: CONGRESS AND THE NATIONAL ECONOMY   25

B. Doctrinal Fundamentals: Federalism and Judicial Review   25
C. The Evolution of the Commerce Clause Doctrine   25
D. State Regulation of Interstate Commerce   27
E. Preemption   28

III. THE SCOPE OF CONGRESS'S POWERS: TAXING AND SPENDING, WAR POWERS, INDIVIDUAL RIGHTS, AND STATE AUTONOMY   29

A. Regulation Through Taxing, Spending, and the War Power   29
B. Congress's Enforcement Powers under the Reconstruction Amendments   30
C. The Tenth Amendment as a Federalism-Based Limitation on Congressional Power   32

| IV. | THE DISTRIBUTION OF NATIONAL POWERS | 35 |

| C. | Foreign Affairs | 35 |
| D. | Domestic Affairs | 36 |

| V. | EQUALITY AND THE CONSTITUTION | 41 |

C.	Equal Protection Methodology: Heightened Scrutiny and the Problem of Race	41
	Fisher v. University of Texas	*41*
	Schuette v. Coalition to Defend Affirmative Action, Integration & Immigrant Rights & Fight for Equality by Any Means Necessary (BAMN)	*48*
E.	The Problem of Sexual Orientation	65
F.	Other Candidates for Heightened Scrutiny	67

| VI. | IMPLIED FUNDAMENTAL RIGHTS | 69 |

F.	Modern Substantive Due Process: Privacy, Personhood, and Family	69
	2. Abortion	69
	3. Family and Other Privacy Interests	69
	United States v. Windsor	69
H.	The Contracts and Takings Clauses	82

| VII. | FREEDOM OF EXPRESSION | 87 |

A.	Introduction	87
B.	Content-Based Restrictions: Dangerous Ideas and Information	87
D.	Content-Based Restrictions: "Low" Value	91
E.	Content-Neutral Restrictions	95
	Agency for International Development v. Alliance for Open Society International	*100*
	McCutcheon v. Federal Election Commission	104
F.	Freedom of the Press	115

VIII. THE CONSTITUTION AND RELIGION 117

A.	Introduction: Historical and Analytical Overview	117
B.	The Establishment Clause	117
D.	Permissible Accommodation	121

IX. STATE ACTION, BASELINES, AND THE PROBLEM OF PRIVATE POWER 123

A.	State Action, Federalism, and Individual Autonomy	123
E.	Unconstitutional Conditions and the Benefit/Burden Distinction	124

Table of Cases

Italics indicate principal and intermediate cases.
All references are to page numbers in the main volume.

Abrams v. United States, 1053
Agency for International Development v. Alliance for Open Society International, 1337, 1418, 1620
Alvarez, United States v., 1263
Arizona v. United States, 290
Arkansas Game & Fish Comm'n v. United States, 1003, 1013
Bond v. United States, 199, 348
Branzburg v. Hayes, 1426
Brown v. Board of Educ., 612
Brown v. Entertainment Merchants Ass'n, 1214, 1263
Brown v. Socialist Workers '74 Campaign Comm'n, 1426
Burwell v. Hobby Lobby Stores, 1549
Chaplinsky v. New Hampshire, 1263
Clapper v. Amnesty International USA, 106
Debs v. United States, 1052
Dolan v. City of Tigard, 1011
Federal Election Comm'n v. Akins, 118
Fisher v. University of Texas, 598
Frohwerk v. United States, 1052
Gonzales v. O Centro Espirita Beneficente Uniao do Vegetal, 1549
Gratz v. Bollinger, 598
Greece, Town of, v. Galloway, 1494
Grutter v. Bollinger, 598
Harris v. Quinn, 1418
Hollingsworth v. Perry, 118
Hopwood v. Texas, 598
Immigration & Naturalization Serv. (INS) v. Chadha, 435
Kebodeaux, United States v., 217
Koontz v. St. Johns River Water Mgmt. Dist., 1011, 1613
Lane v. Franks, 1404
Lawrence v. Texas, 1192, 1201
Lexmark Intl. v. Static Control Components, 107
McBurney v. Young, 263

McCullen v. Coakley, 1274, 1281
McCutcheon v. Federal Election Commission, 1400
McIntyre v. Ohio Election Comm'n, 1426
NAACP v. Alabama, 1426
National Fed'n of Indep. Bus. v. Sebelius, 239, 1561
National Labor Relations Bd. v. Noel Canning, 451
Nollan v. California Coastal Comm'n, 1011, 1613
Northwestern Austin Mun. Util. Dist. No. 1 v. Holder, 335
O'Brien v. United States, 1426
Planned Parenthood of Se. Pa. v. Casey, 1201
Regents of Univ. of Cal. v. Bakke, 598
Reliable Consultants, Inc. v. Earl, 1192, 1201
Richards, United States v., 1211
Roe v. Wade, 1201
Rumsfeld v. FAIR, 1011
Schenck v. United States, 1052
Schuette v. Coalition to Defend Affirmative Action, Integration & Immigrant Rights & Fight for Equality by Any Means Necessary (BAMN), 624, 628
Shelby Cnty. v. Holder, 335
Snyder v. Phelps, 1011, 1214, 1263
Stevens, United States v., 1211, 1214, 1263
Susan B. Anthony List v. Driehaus, 106
Talley v. California, 1426
Town of _____ v. *See* name of town
Windsor, United States v., 118, 215, 689, *937*
Windsor v. United States, 689
Yates v. United States, 1070

Table of Authorities

Abrams, Plenary Power Preemption, 99 Va. L. Rev. 601 (2013), 290
Ackerman, B., The Decline and Fall of the American Republic (2010), 423
Ashdown, Distorting Democracy: Campaign Lies in the 21st Century, 20 Wm. & Mary Bill Rts. J. 1085 (2012), 1149
Bhagwat, Details: Specific Facts and the First Amendment, 86 S. Cal. L. Rev. 1 (2012), 1112
Bradley & Morrison, Historical Gloss and the Separation of Powers, 126 Harv. L. Rev. 411 (2012), 389
Bradley & Morrison, Presidential Power, Historical Practice, and Legal Constraint, 113 Colum. L. Rev. 1097 (2013), 423
Brudney, The First Amendment and Commercial Advertising, 53 B.C. L. Rev. 1153 (2013), 1173, 1180
Cashin, S., Place not Race: A New Vision of Opportunity in America (2014), 598
Coenen, Of Speech and Sanctions: Toward a Penalty-Sensitive Approach to the First Amendment, 112 Colum. L. Rev. 991 (2012), 1053
Collins, R., & D. Skover, On Dissent: Its Meaning in America (2013), 1035
Collins, Exceptional Freedom: The Roberts Court, the First Amendment, and the New Absolutism, 76 Alb. L. Rev. 409 (2013), 1263
Feature, Federalism as the New Nationalism, 123 Yale L.J. 1888 (2014), 175
Friedman & Lakier, "To Regulate," Not "To Prohibit": Limiting the Commerce Power, 2012 Sup. Ct. Rev. 255 (2013), 185
Healy, T., The Great Dissent: How Oliver Wendell Holmes Changed His Mind—and Changed the History of Free Speech in America (2013), 1052
Hellman, Defining Corruption and Constitutionalizing Democracy, 111 Mich. L. Rev. 1385 (2013), 1400
Heyman, To Drink the Cup of Fury: Funeral Picketing, Public Discourse, and the First Amendment, 45 Conn. L. Rev. 101 (2012), 1100
Jones, Rethinking Reporter's Privilege, 111 Mich. L. Rev. 1221 (2013), 1426
Kalven, H., A Worthy Tradition: Freedom of Speech in America (1988), 1263
Kendrick, Speech, Intent, and the Chilling Effect, 54 Wm. & Mary L. Rev. 1633 (2013), 1142
Kinsley, Sexual Privacy in the Internet Age: How Substantive Due Process Protects Online Obscenity, 16 Vand. J. Ent. & Tech. L. 103 (2013), 1192, 1201
Koppelman, Defending American Religious Neutrality (2013), 1467
Koppelman, The New American Civil Religion: Lessons for Italy, Geo. Wash. Int'l L. Rev. 961 (2010), 1499

Leiter, Why Tolerate Religion? (2012), 1467

Lessig, What an Originalist Would Understand "Corruption" to Mean, 102 Cal. L. Rev. 1 (2014), 1400

Lichman, R., The Supreme Court and McCarthy Era Repression: One Hundred Decisions (2012), 1112

Norton, The Equal Protection Implications of Government's Hateful Speech, 54 Wm. & Mary L. Rev. 159 (2012), 1334

Norton, Lies and the Constitution, 2012 Sup. Ct. Rev. 161, 1153

Note, NFIB v. Sebelius and the Individualization of the State Action Doctrine, 127 Harv. L. Rev. 1174 (2014), 1561

Persilly, Metzger, & Morrison, eds., The Health Care Case: The Supreme Court's Decision and Its Implications (2013), 239

Pollvogt, Beyond Suspect Classifications, 16 U. Pa. J. Const. L. 739 (2014), 719

Posner, E., & A. Vermeule, The Executive Unbound: After the Madisonian Re public (2010), 423

Post, R., Citizens Divided: Campaign Finance Reform and the Constitution (2014), 1400

Rosen & Schmidt, Why Broccoli?: Limiting Principles and Popular Constitutionalism in the Health Care Case, 61 UCLA L. Rev. 66 (2013), 239

Schauer, Harm(s) and the First Amendment, 2011 Sup. Ct. Rev. 81, 1214

Schwartzman, What If Religion Is Not Special, 79 U. Chi. L. Rev. 1351 (2012), 1467

Siegel, Foreword: Equality Divided, 127 Harv. L. Rev. 1 (2013), 628

Siegel, The REINS Act and the Struggle to Control Agency Rulemaking, 116 N.Y.U. J. Legis. & Pub. Pol'y 131 (2013), 435

Stevens, J.P., Six Amendments: How and Why We Should Change the Constitution (2014), 1400

Stone, G., Top Secret: When Government Keeps Us in the Dark (2007), 1426

Tarkington, A First Amendment Theory for Protecting Attorney Speech, 45 U.C. Davis L. Rev. 27 (2011), 1078

Tribe, L., & J. Matz, Uncertain Justice: The Roberts Court and the Constitution (2014), 1078, 1400

THE SUPREME COURT SINCE 1789

Page lxxxviii. Justices Sotomayor and Kagan are listed in the wrong column of the chart. Justice Sotomayor was appointed to replace Justice Souter. Justice Kagan was appointed to replace Justice Stevens.

I
THE CONSTITUTION AND THE SUPREME COURT

F. *"Case or Controversy" Requirements and the Passive Virtues*

2. Standing

Page 106. Before the Note, add the following:

CLAPPER v. AMNESTY INTERNATIONAL USA
133 S. Ct. 1138 (2013)

JUSTICE ALITO delivered the opinion of the Court.

Section 702 of the Foreign Intelligence Surveillance Act of 1978, 50 U.S.C. § 1881a (2006 ed., Supp. V), allows the Attorney General and the Director of National Intelligence to acquire foreign intelligence information by jointly authorizing the surveillance of individuals who are not "United States persons" and are reasonably believed to be located outside the United States. Before doing so, the Attorney General and the Director of National Intelligence normally must obtain the Foreign Intelligence Surveillance Court's approval. Respondents are United States persons whose work, they allege, requires them to engage in sensitive international communications with individuals who they believe are likely targets of surveillance under § 1881a. Respondents seek a declaration that § 1881a is unconstitutional, as well as an injunction against § 1881a-authorized surveillance. The question before us is whether respondents have Article III standing to seek this prospective relief.

Respondents assert that they can establish injury in fact because there is an objectively reasonable likelihood that their communications will be acquired under § 1881a at some point in the future. But respondents' theory of *future* injury is too speculative to satisfy the well-established requirement that threatened injury must be "certainly impending." And even if respondents could demonstrate that the threatened injury is certainly impending, they still would not be able to establish that this injury is fairly traceable to § 1881a. As an alternative argument, respondents contend that they are suffering *present* injury because the risk of § 1881a-authorized surveillance already has forced them to take costly and burdensome measures to protect the confidentiality of their international communications. But respondents cannot manufacture standing by choosing to make expenditures based on hypothetical future harm that is not certainly impending. We therefore hold that respondents lack Article III standing.

I

A ...

The present case involves a constitutional challenge to § 1881a. Surveillance under § 1881a is subject to statutory conditions, judicial authorization, congressional supervision, and compliance with the Fourth Amendment. Section 1881a provides that, upon the issuance of an order from the Foreign Intelligence Surveillance Court [FISC], "the Attorney General and the Director of National Intelligence may authorize jointly, for a period of up to 1 year . . . , the targeting of persons reasonably believed to be located outside the United States to acquire foreign intelligence information." Surveillance under § 1881a may not be intentionally targeted at any person known to be in the United States or any U.S. person reasonably believed to be located abroad. Additionally, acquisitions under § 1881a must comport with the Fourth Amendment. Moreover, surveillance under § 1881a is subject to congressional oversight and several types of Executive Branch review.

Section 1881a mandates that the Government obtain the Foreign Intelligence Surveillance Court's approval of "targeting" procedures, "minimization" procedures, and a governmental certification regarding proposed surveillance. Among other things, the Government's certification must attest that (1) procedures are in place "that have been approved, have been submitted for approval, or will be submitted with the certification for approval by the [FISC] that are reasonably designed" to ensure that an acquisition is "limited to targeting persons reasonably believed to be located outside" the United States; (2) minimization procedures adequately restrict the acquisition, retention, and dissemination of nonpublic information about unconsenting U.S. persons, as appropriate; (3) guidelines have been adopted to ensure compliance with targeting limits and the Fourth Amendment; and (4) the procedures and guidelines referred to above comport with the Fourth Amendment.

The Foreign Intelligence Surveillance Court's role includes determining whether the Government's certification contains the required elements . . .

B

Respondents are attorneys and human rights, labor, legal, and media organizations whose work allegedly requires them to engage in sensitive and sometimes privileged telephone and e-mail communications with colleagues, clients, sources, and other individuals located abroad. [Respondents] claim that they communicate by telephone and e-mail with people the Government "believes or believed to be associated with terrorist organizations," "people located in geographic areas that are a special focus" of the Government's counterterrorism or diplomatic efforts, and activists who oppose governments that are supported by the United States Government.

Respondents claim that § 1881a compromises their ability to locate witnesses, cultivate sources, obtain information, and communicate confidential information to their clients. Respondents also assert that they "have ceased engaging" in certain telephone and e-mail conversations. According to respondents, the threat of surveillance will compel them to travel abroad in order to have in-person conversations. In addition, respondents declare that they have undertaken "costly and burdensome measures" to protect the confidentiality of sensitive communications. . . .

III

A

Respondents assert that they can establish injury in fact that is fairly traceable to § 1881a because there is an objectively reasonable likelihood that their communications with their foreign contacts will be intercepted under § 1881a at some point in the future. This argument fails. . . .

[Respondents'] argument rests on their highly speculative fear that: (1) the Government will decide to target the communications of non-U.S. persons with whom they communicate; (2) in doing so, the Government will choose to invoke its authority under § 1881a rather than utilizing another method of surveillance; (3) the Article III judges who serve on the Foreign Intelligence Surveillance Court will conclude that the Government's proposed surveillance procedures satisfy § 1881a's many safeguards and are consistent with the Fourth Amendment; (4) the Government will succeed in intercepting the communications of respondents' contacts; and (5) respondents will be parties to the particular communications that the Government intercepts. . . .

[Respondents'] theory of standing, which relies on a highly attenuated chain of possibilities, does not satisfy the requirement that threatened injury must be certainly impending. Moreover, even if respondents could demonstrate injury in fact, the second link in the above-described chain of contingencies — which amounts to mere speculation about whether surveillance would be under § 1881a or some other authority — shows that respondents cannot satisfy the requirement that any injury in fact must be fairly traceable to § 1881a.

First, it is speculative whether the Government will imminently target communications to which respondents are parties. Section 1881a expressly provides that respondents, who are U.S. persons, cannot be targeted for surveillance under § 1881a. . . .

Accordingly, respondents' theory necessarily rests on their assertion that the Government will target *other individuals*—namely, their foreign contacts.

Yet respondents have no actual knowledge of the Government's § 1881a targeting practices. Instead, respondents merely speculate and make assumptions about whether their communications with their foreign contacts will be acquired under § 1881a. For example, journalist Christopher Hedges states: "I have no choice but to *assume* that any of my international communications *may* be subject to government surveillance, and I have to make decisions . . . in light of that *assumption*." Similarly, attorney Scott McKay asserts that, "[b]ecause of the [FISA Amendments Act], we now have to *assume* that every one of our international communications *may* be monitored by the government." . . .

[Because] § 1881a at most *authorizes*—but does not *mandate* or *direct*—the surveillance that respondents fear, respondents' allegations are necessarily conjectural. Simply put, respondents can only speculate as to how the Attorney General and the Director of National Intelligence will exercise their discretion in determining which communications to target.

Second, even if respondents could demonstrate that the targeting of their foreign contacts is imminent, respondents can only speculate as to whether the Government will seek to use § 1881 authorized surveillance (rather than other methods) to do so. The Government has numerous other methods of conducting surveillance, none of which is challenged here. Even after the enactment of the FISA Amendments Act, for example, the Government may still conduct electronic surveillance of persons abroad under the older provisions of FISA so long as it satisfies the applicable requirements, including a demonstration of probable cause to believe that the person is a foreign power or agent of a foreign power. The Government may also obtain information from the intelligence services of foreign nations. . . . Even if respondents could demonstrate that their foreign contacts will imminently be targeted—indeed, even if they could show that interception of their own communications will imminently occur—they would still need to show that their injury is fairly traceable to § 1881a. But, because respondents can only speculate as to whether any (asserted) interception would be under § 1881a or some other authority, they cannot satisfy the "fairly traceable" requirement.

Third, even if respondents could show that the Government will seek the Foreign Intelligence Surveillance Court's authorization to acquire the communications of respondents' foreign contacts under § 1881a, respondents can only speculate as to whether that court will authorize such surveillance. . . .

We decline to abandon our usual reluctance to endorse standing theories that rest on speculation about the decisions of independent actors. In sum, respondents' speculative chain of possibilities does not establish that injury based on potential future surveillance is certainly impending or is fairly traceable to § 1881a.

B

Respondents' alternative argument—namely, that they can establish standing based on the measures that they have undertaken to avoid § 1881a-authorized surveillance—fares no better. Respondents assert that they are suffering ongoing injuries that are fairly traceable to § 1881a because the risk of surveillance under § 1881a requires them to take costly and burdensome measures to protect the confidentiality of their communications. Respondents claim, for instance, that the threat of surveillance sometimes compels them to avoid certain e-mail and phone conversations, to "tal[k] in generalities rather than specifics," or to travel so that they can have in-person conversations. . . .

Respondents' contention that they have standing because they incurred certain costs as a reasonable reaction to a risk of harm is unavailing—because the harm respondents seek to avoid is not certainly impending. In other words, respondents cannot manufacture standing merely by inflicting harm on themselves based on their fears of hypothetical future harm that is not certainly impending. Any ongoing injuries that respondents are suffering are not fairly traceable to § 1881a.

If the law were otherwise, an enterprising plaintiff would be able to secure a lower standard for Article III standing simply by making an expenditure based on a nonparanoid fear. . . .

Thus, allowing respondents to bring this action based on costs they incurred in response to a speculative threat would be tantamount to accepting a repackaged version of respondents' first failed theory of standing.

Another reason that respondents' present injuries are not fairly traceable to § 1881a is that even before § 1881a was enacted, they had a similar incentive to engage in many of the countermeasures that they are now taking. . . .

IV

A

Respondents incorrectly maintain that "[t]he kinds of injuries incurred here—injuries incurred because of [respondents'] reasonable efforts to avoid greater injuries that are otherwise likely to flow from the conduct they challenge—are the same kinds of injuries that this Court held to support standing in cases such as" *Laidlaw* [and] Meese v. Keene, 481 U.S. 465 (1987). . . .

[Each] of these cases was very different from the present case.

In *Laidlaw*, plaintiffs' standing was based on "the proposition that a company's continuous and pervasive illegal discharges of pollutants into a river would cause nearby residents to curtail their recreational use of that waterway and would subject them to other economic and aesthetic harms." Because the unlawful discharges of pollutants were "concededly ongoing," the only issue was whether "nearby residents"—who were members of the organizational plaintiffs—acted reasonably in refraining from using the polluted area. *Laidlaw* is therefore quite unlike the present case, in which it is not "concede[d]" that respondents would be subject to unlawful surveillance but for their decision to take preventive measures. *Laidlaw* would resemble this case only if (1) it were undisputed that the Government was using § 1881a-authorized surveillance to acquire respondents' communications and (2) the sole dispute concerned the reasonableness of respondents' preventive measures.

In *Keene*, the plaintiff challenged the constitutionality of the Government's decision to label three films as "political propaganda." The Court held that the plaintiff, who was an attorney and a state legislator, had standing because he demonstrated, through "detailed affidavits," that he "could not exhibit the films without incurring a risk of injury to his reputation and of an impairment of his political career." Unlike the present case, *Keene* involved "more than a 'subjective chill'" based on speculation about potential governmental action; the plaintiff in that case was unquestionably regulated by the relevant statute, and the films that he wished to exhibit had already been labeled as "political propaganda." . . .

B

Respondents also suggest that they should be held to have standing because otherwise the constitutionality of § 1881a could not be challenged. It would be wrong, they maintain, to "insulate the government's surveillance activities from meaningful judicial review." Respondents' suggestion is both legally and factually incorrect. First, "'[t]he assumption that if respondents have no standing to sue, no one would have standing, is not a reason to find standing.'"

Second, our holding today by no means insulates § 1881a from judicial review. As described above, Congress created a comprehensive scheme in which the Foreign Intelligence Surveillance Court evaluates the Government's certifications, targeting procedures, and minimization procedures—including assessing whether the targeting and minimization procedures comport with the Fourth Amendment. Any dissatisfaction that respondents may have about the Foreign Intelligence Surveillance Court's rulings—or the congressional delineation of that court's role—is irrelevant to our standing analysis.

Additionally, if the Government intends to use or disclose information obtained or derived from a § 1881a acquisition in judicial or administrative proceedings, it must provide advance notice of its intent, and the affected person may challenge the lawfulness of the acquisition. . . .

Finally, any electronic communications service provider that the Government directs to assist in § 1881a surveillance may challenge the lawfulness of that directive before the FISC. Indeed, at the behest of a service provider, the Foreign Intelligence Surveillance Court of Review previously analyzed the constitutionality of electronic surveillance directives issued pursuant to a now-expired set of FISA amendments.

* * *

We hold that respondents lack Article III standing because they cannot demonstrate that the future injury they purportedly fear is certainly impending and because they cannot manufacture standing by incurring costs in anticipation of non-imminent harm. We therefore reverse the judgment of the Second Circuit and remand the case for further proceedings consistent with this opinion.

It is so ordered.

JUSTICE BREYER, with whom JUSTICE GINSBURG, JUSTICE SOTOMAYOR, and JUSTICE KAGAN join, dissenting.

I . . .

No one here denies that the Government's interception of a private telephone or e-mail conversation amounts to an injury that is "concrete and particularized." Moreover, the plaintiffs, respondents here, seek as relief a judgment declaring unconstitutional (and enjoining enforcement of) a statutory provision authorizing those interceptions; and, such a judgment would redress the injury by preventing it. Thus, the basic question is whether the injury, *i.e.,* the interception, is "actual or imminent."

II

A . . .

The addition of § 1881a in 2008 changed [prior] law in three important ways. First, it eliminated the requirement that the Government describe to the court each specific target and identify each facility at which its surveillance would be directed, thus permitting surveillance on a programmatic, not necessarily individualized, basis. Second, it eliminated the requirement that a target be a "foreign power or an agent of a foreign power." Third, it diminished the court's authority to insist upon, and eliminated its authority to supervise, instance-specific privacy-intrusion minimization procedures (though the Government still must use court-approved general minimization procedures). Thus, using the authority of § 1881a, the Government can obtain court approval for its surveillance of electronic communications between places within the United States and targets in foreign territories by showing the court (1) that "a significant purpose of the acquisition is to obtain foreign intelligence information," and (2) that it will use general targeting and privacy-intrusion minimization procedures of a kind that the court had previously approved.

B...
Plaintiff Scott McKay [says] in an affidavit (1) that he is a lawyer; (2) that he represented "Mr. Sami Omar Al-Hussayen, who was acquitted in June 2004 on terrorism charges"; (3) that he continues to represent "Mr. Al-Hussayen, who, in addition to facing criminal charges after September 11, was named as a defendant in several civil cases"; (4) that he represents Khalid Sheik Mohammed, a detainee, "before the Military Commissions at Guantanamo Bay, Cuba"; (5) that in representing these clients he "communicate[s] by telephone and email with people outside the United States, including Mr. Al-Hussayen himself," "experts, investigators, attorneys, family members . . . and others who are located abroad"; and (6) that prior to 2008 "the U.S. government had intercepted some 10,000 telephone calls and 20,000 email communications involving [his client] Al-Hussayen." . . .

[Another] plaintiff, Joanne Mariner, says in her affidavit (1) that she is a human rights researcher, (2) that "some of the work [she] do[es] involves trying to track down people who were rendered by the CIA to countries in which they were tortured"; (3) that many of those people "the CIA has said are (or were) associated with terrorist organizations"; and (4) that, to do this research, she "communicate[s] by telephone and e-mail with . . . former detainees, lawyers for detainees, relatives of detainees, political activists, journalists, and fixers" "all over the world, including in Jordan, Egypt, Pakistan, Afghanistan, [and] the Gaza Strip." . . .

III

Several considerations, based upon the record along with commonsense inferences, convince me that there is a very high likelihood that Government, *acting under the authority of* § 1881a, will intercept at least some of the communications just described. First, the plaintiffs have engaged, and continue to engage, in electronic communications of a kind that the 2008 amendment, but not the prior Act, authorizes the Government to intercept. These communications include discussions with family members of those detained at Guantanamo, friends and acquaintances of those persons, and investigators, experts and others with knowledge of circumstances related to terrorist activities. These persons are foreigners located outside the United States. They are not "foreign power[s]" or "agent[s] of . . . foreign power[s]." And the plaintiffs state that they exchange with these persons "foreign intelligence information," defined to include information that

I. The Constitution and the Supreme Court

"relates to" "international terrorism" and "the national defense or the security of the United States."

Second, the plaintiffs have a strong *motive* to engage in, and the Government has a strong *motive* to listen to, conversations of the kind described. A lawyer representing a client normally seeks to learn the circumstances surrounding the crime (or the civil wrong) of which the client is accused. A fair reading of the affidavit of Scott McKay, for example, taken together with elementary considerations of a lawyer's obligation to his client, indicates that McKay will engage in conversations that concern what suspected foreign terrorists, such as his client, have done; in conversations that concern his clients' families, colleagues, and contacts; in conversations that concern what those persons (or those connected to them) have said and done, at least in relation to terrorist activities; in conversations that concern the political, social, and commercial environments in which the suspected terrorists have lived and worked; and so forth. Journalists and human rights workers have strong similar motives to conduct conversations of this kind.

At the same time, the Government has a strong motive to conduct surveillance of conversations that contain material of this kind. The Government, after all, seeks to learn as much as it can reasonably learn about suspected terrorists (such as those detained at Guantanamo), as well as about their contacts and activities, along with those of friends and family members. And the Government is motivated to do so, not simply by the desire to help convict those whom the Government believes guilty, but also by the critical, overriding need to protect America from terrorism.

Third, the Government's *past behavior* shows that it has sought, and hence will in all likelihood continue to seek, information about alleged terrorists and detainees through means that include surveillance of electronic communications. As just pointed out, plaintiff Scott McKay states that the Government (under the authority of the pre-2008 law) "intercepted some 10,000 telephone calls and 20,000 email communications involving [his client] Mr. Al-Hussayen."

Fourth, the Government has the *capacity* to conduct electronic surveillance of the kind at issue. To some degree this capacity rests upon technology available to the Government. [This] capacity also includes the Government's authority to obtain the kind of information here at issue from private carriers such as AT&T and Verizon. We are further told by *amici* that the Government is expanding that capacity.

Of course, to exercise this capacity the Government must have intelligence court authorization. But the Government rarely files requests that fail to meet the statutory criteria. As the intelligence court itself has stated, its review under § 1881a is "narrowly circumscribed." There is no reason to believe that the communications described would all fail to meet the conditions necessary for approval. Moreover, compared with prior law, § 1881a simplifies and thus expedites the approval process, making it more likely that the Government will use § 1881a to obtain the necessary approval.

The upshot is that (1) similarity of content, (2) strong motives, (3) prior behavior, and (4) capacity all point to a very strong likelihood that the Government will intercept at least some of the plaintiffs' communications, including some that the 2008 amendment, § 1881a, but not the pre-2008 Act, authorizes the Government to intercept. . . .

Consequently, we need only assume that the Government is doing its job (to find out about, and combat, terrorism) in order to conclude that there is a high probability that the Government will intercept at least some electronic communication to which at least some of the plaintiffs are parties. The majority is wrong when it describes the harm threatened plaintiffs as "speculative."

IV

A

The majority more plausibly says that the plaintiffs have failed to show that the threatened harm is *"certainly impending."* But [*certainty*] is not, and never has been, the touchstone of standing. The future is inherently uncertain. Yet federal courts frequently entertain actions for injunctions and for declaratory relief aimed at preventing future activities that are reasonably likely or highly likely, but not absolutely certain, to take place. And that degree of certainty is all that is needed to support standing here.

The Court's use of the term "certainly impending" is not to the contrary. . . .

Taken together the case law uses the word "certainly" as if it emphasizes, rather than literally defines, the immediately following term "impending."

B

1

More important, the Court's holdings in standing cases show that standing exists here. The Court has often *found* standing where the occurrence of the relevant injury was far *less* certain than here. Consider a few, fairly typical, cases. Consider *Pennell.* A city ordinance forbade landlords to raise the rent charged to a tenant by more than 8 percent where doing so would work an unreasonably severe hardship on that tenant. A group of landlords sought a judgment declaring the ordinance unconstitutional. The Court held that, to have standing, the landlords had to demonstrate a "'*realistic danger of sustaining a direct injury* as a result of the statute's operation.'" It found that the landlords had done so by showing a likelihood of enforcement and a "probability," that the ordinance would make the landlords charge lower rents—even though the landlords had not shown (1) that they intended to raise the relevant rents to the point of causing unreasonably severe hardship; (2) that the tenants would challenge those increases; or (3) that the city's hearing examiners and arbitrators would find against the landlords.

Here, even more so than in *Pennell*, there is a *"realistic danger"* that the relevant harm will occur....

How could the law be otherwise? Suppose that a federal court faced a claim by homeowners that (allegedly) unlawful dam-building practices created a high risk that their homes would be flooded. Would the court deny them standing on the ground that the risk of flood was only 60, rather than 90, percent?

Would federal courts deny standing to a plaintiff in a diversity action who claims an anticipatory breach of contract where the future breach depends on probabilities? The defendant, say, has threatened to load wheat onto a ship bound for India despite a promise to send the wheat to the United States. No one can know for certain that this will happen. Perhaps the defendant will change his mind; perhaps the ship will turn and head for the United States. Yet, despite the uncertainty, the Constitution does not prohibit a federal court from hearing such a claim....

Neither do ordinary declaratory judgment actions always involve the degree of certainty upon which the Court insists here. See, *e.g.*, . . . Aetna Life Ins. Co. v. Haworth, 300 U.S. 227, 239-244 (1937).

2

In some standing cases, the Court has found that a reasonable probability of *future* injury comes accompanied with *present* injury that takes the form of reasonable efforts to mitigate the threatened effects of the future injury or to prevent it from occurring....

Virtually identical circumstances are present here. Plaintiff McKay, for example, points out that, when he communicates abroad about, or in the interests of, a client (*e.g.*, a client accused of terrorism), he must "make an assessment" whether his "client's interests would be compromised" should the Government "acquire the communications." If so, he must either forgo the communication or travel abroad....

4

In sum [the] word "certainly" in the phrase "certainly impending" does not refer to absolute certainty. As our case law demonstrates, what the Constitution requires is something more akin to "reasonable probability" or "high probability." The use of some such standard is all that is necessary here to ensure the actual concrete injury that the Constitution demands. The considerations set forth in Parts II and III, *supra*, make clear that the standard is readily met in this case.

* * *

While I express no view on the merits of the plaintiffs' constitutional claims, I do believe that at least some of the plaintiffs have standing to make those claims. I dissent, with respect, from the majority's contrary conclusion.

SUSAN B. ANTHONY LIST v. DRIEHAUS

134 S. Ct. 2334 (2014)

JUSTICE THOMAS delivered the opinion of the Court.

Petitioners in this case seek to challenge an Ohio statute that prohibits certain "false statements" during the course of a political campaign. The question in this case is whether their preenforcement challenge to that law is justiciable—and in particular, whether they have alleged a sufficiently imminent injury for the purposes of Article III. We conclude that they have.

I

The Ohio statute at issue prohibits certain "false statement[s]" "during the course of any campaign for nomination or election to public office or office of a political party." As relevant here, the statute makes it a crime for any person to "[m]ake a false statement concerning the voting record of a candidate or public official," or to "[p]ost, publish, circulate, distribute, or otherwise disseminate a false statement concerning a candidate, either knowing the same to be false or with reckless disregard of whether it was false or not." "[A]ny person" acting on personal knowledge may file a complaint with the Ohio Elections Commission (or Commission) alleging a violation of the false statement statute. If filed within 60 days of a primary election or 90 days of a general election, the complaint is referred to a panel of at least three Commission members. The panel must then hold an expedited hearing, generally within two business days, to determine whether there is probable cause to believe the alleged violation occurred. Upon a finding of probable cause, the full Commission must, within 10 days, hold a hearing on the complaint. . . .

II

Petitioner Susan B. Anthony List (SBA) is a "pro-life advocacy organization." During the 2010 election cycle, SBA publicly criticized various Members of Congress who voted for the Patient Protection and Affordable Care Act (ACA). In particular, it issued a press release announcing its plan to "educat[e] voters that their representative voted for a health care bill that includes taxpayer-funded abortion." The press release listed then-Congressman Steve Driehaus, a respondent here, who voted for the ACA. SBA also sought to display a billboard in Driehaus' district condemning that vote. The planned billboard would have read: "Shame on Steve Driehaus! Driehaus voted FOR taxpayer-funded abortion." The advertising company that owned the billboard space refused to display that message, however, after Driehaus' counsel threatened legal action.

I. The Constitution and the Supreme Court

On October 4, 2010, Driehaus filed a complaint with the Ohio Elections Commission alleging, as relevant here, that SBA had violated [the statute] by falsely stating that he had voted for "taxpayer-funded abortion." Because Driehaus filed his complaint 29 days before the general election, a Commission panel held an expedited hearing. On October 14, 2010, the panel voted 2 to 1 to find probable cause that a violation had been committed. The full Commission set a hearing date for 10 business days later, and the parties commenced discovery. Driehaus noticed depositions of three SBA employees as well as individuals affiliated with similar advocacy groups. He also issued discovery requests for all evidence that SBA would rely on at the Commission hearing, as well as SBA's communications with allied organizations, political party committees, and Members of Congress and their staffs.

On October 18, 2010—after the panel's probable-cause determination, but before the scheduled Commission hearing—SBA filed suit in Federal District Court, seeking declaratory and injunctive relief on the ground that [the statute] violate[s] the First and Fourteenth Amendments of the United States Constitution. The District Court stayed the action under Younger v. Harris, 401 U.S. 37 (1971), pending completion of the Commission proceedings. The Sixth Circuit denied SBA's motion for an injunction pending appeal. Driehaus and SBA eventually agreed to postpone the full Commission hearing until after the election.

When Driehaus lost the election in November 2010, he moved to withdraw his complaint against SBA. The Commission granted the motion with SBA's consent. Once the Commission proceedings were terminated, the District Court lifted the stay and SBA amended its complaint. As relevant here, the amended complaint alleged that [the statute is] unconstitutional both facially and as applied. Specifically, the complaint alleged that SBA's speech about Driehaus had been chilled; that SBA "intends to engage in substantially similar activity in the future"; and that it "face[d] the prospect of its speech and associational rights again being chilled and burdened," because "[a]ny complainant can hale [it] before the [Commission], forcing it to expend time and resources defending itself."

The District Court consolidated SBA's suit with a separate suit brought by petitioner Coalition Opposed to Additional Spending and Taxes (COAST), an advocacy organization that also alleged that the same Ohio false statement provisions are unconstitutional both facially and as applied. According to its amended complaint, COAST intended to disseminate a mass e-mail and other materials criticizing Driehaus' vote for the ACA as a vote "to fund abortions with tax dollars," but refrained from doing so because of the Commission proceedings against SBA. COAST further alleged that it "desires to make the same or similar statements about other federal candidates who voted for" the ACA, but that fear "of finding itself subject to the same fate" as SBA has deterred it from doing so. . . .

III

A

[This] case concerns the injury-in-fact requirement, which helps to ensure that the plaintiff has a "personal stake in the outcome of the controversy." Warth v. Seldin, 422 U.S. 490, 498 (1975) (internal quotation marks omitted). An injury sufficient to satisfy Article III must be "concrete and particularized" and "actual or imminent, not 'conjectural' or 'hypothetical.'" [*Lujan.*] An allegation of future injury may suffice if the threatened injury is "certainly impending," or there is a "'substantial risk' that the harm will occur." [*Clapper.*]

B

One recurring issue in our cases is determining when the threatened enforcement of a law creates an Article III injury. When an individual is subject to such a threat, an actual arrest, prosecution, or other enforcement action is not a prerequisite to challenging the law. . . .

IV

Here, SBA and COAST contend that the threat of enforcement of the false statement statute amounts to an Article III injury in fact. We agree: Petitioners have alleged a credible threat of enforcement.

A

First, petitioners have alleged "an intention to engage in a course of conduct arguably affected with a constitutional interest." Both petitioners have pleaded specific statements they intend to make in future election cycles. SBA has already stated that representatives who voted for the ACA supported "taxpayer-funded abortion," and it has alleged an "inten[t] to engage in substantially similar activity in the future." COAST has alleged that it previously intended to disseminate materials criticizing a vote for the ACA as a vote "to fund abortions with tax dollars," and that it "desires to make the same or similar statements about other federal candidates who voted for [the ACA]." Because petitioners' intended future conduct concerns political speech, it is certainly "affected with a constitutional interest."

B

Next, petitioners' intended future conduct is "arguably . . . proscribed by [the] statute" they wish to challenge. The Ohio false statement law sweeps broadly, and covers the subject matter of petitioners' intended speech. Both SBA and COAST have alleged an intent to "[m]ake" statements "concerning the voting record of a candidate or public official," and to "disseminate" statements "concerning a candidate . . . to promote the election, nomination, or defeat of the candidate[.]" And, a Commission panel here already found probable cause to believe that SBA violated the statute when it stated that Driehaus had supported "taxpayer-funded abortion"—the same sort of statement petitioners plan to disseminate in the future. Under these circumstances, we have no difficulty concluding that petitioners' intended speech is "arguably proscribed" by the law.

Respondents incorrectly rely on Golden v. Zwickler, 394 U.S. 103 (1969). In that case, the plaintiff had previously distributed anonymous leaflets criticizing a particular Congressman who had since left office. The Court dismissed the plaintiff's challenge to the electoral leafletting ban as nonjusticiable because his "*sole concern* was literature relating to the Congressman and his record," and "it was most unlikely that the Congressman would again be a candidate." (emphasis added). Under those circumstances, any threat of future prosecution was "wholly conjectural."

Here, by contrast, petitioners' speech focuses on the broader issue of support for the ACA, not on the voting record of a single candidate. Because petitioners' alleged future speech is not directed exclusively at Driehaus, it does not matter whether he "may run for office again." As long as petitioners continue to engage in comparable electoral speech regarding support for the ACA, that speech will remain arguably proscribed by Ohio's false statement statute.

Respondents, echoing the Sixth Circuit, contend that SBA's fears of enforcement are misplaced because SBA has not said it "'plans to lie or recklessly disregard the veracity of its speech.'" The Sixth Circuit reasoned that because SBA "can only be liable for making a statement 'knowing' it is false," SBA's insistence that its speech is factually true "makes the possibility of prosecution for uttering such statements exceedingly slim."

The Sixth Circuit misses the point. SBA's insistence that the allegations in its press release were true did not prevent the Commission panel from finding probable cause to believe that SBA had violated the law the first time around. And, there is every reason to think that similar speech in the future will result in similar proceedings, notwithstanding SBA's belief in the truth of its allegations. Nothing in this Court's decisions requires a plaintiff who wishes to challenge the constitutionality of a law to confess that he will in fact violate that law.

C

Finally, the threat of future enforcement of the false statement statute is substantial. Most obviously, there is a history of past enforcement here. . . .

[Commission] proceedings are not a rare occurrence. Petitioners inform us that the Commission "'handles about 20 to 80 false statement complaints per year,'" and respondents do not deny that the Commission frequently fields complaints alleging violations of the false statement statute. Moreover, respondents have not disavowed enforcement if petitioners make similar statements in the future. In fact, the specter of enforcement is so substantial that the owner of the billboard refused to display SBA's message after receiving a letter threatening Commission proceedings. On these facts, the prospect of future enforcement is far from "imaginary or speculative."

We take the threatened Commission proceedings into account because administrative action, like arrest or prosecution, may give rise to harm sufficient to justify pre-enforcement review. The burdens that Commission proceedings can impose on electoral speech are of particular concern here. As the Ohio Attorney General himself notes, the "practical effect" of the Ohio false statement scheme is "to permit a private complainant . . . to gain a campaign advantage without ever having to prove the falsity of a statement." [Moreover], the target of a false statement complaint may be forced to divert significant time and resources to hire legal counsel and respond to discovery requests in the crucial days leading up to an election. And where, as here, a Commission panel issues a preelection probable-cause finding, "such a determination itself may be viewed [by the electorate] as a sanction by the State."

Although the threat of Commission proceedings is a substantial one, we need not decide whether that threat standing alone gives rise to an Article III injury. The burdensome Commission proceedings here are backed by the additional threat of criminal prosecution. We conclude that the combination of those two threats suffices to create an Article III injury under the circumstances of this case.

That conclusion holds true as to both SBA and COAST. Respondents, relying on Younger v. Harris, 401 U.S. 37 (1971), appear to suggest that COAST lacks standing because it refrained from actually disseminating its planned speech in order to avoid Commission proceedings of its own. In *Younger,* the plaintiff had been indicted for distributing leaflets in violation of the California Criminal Syndicalism Act. When he challenged the constitutionality of the law in federal court, several other plaintiffs intervened, arguing that their own speech was inhibited by Harris' prosecution. The Court concluded that only the plaintiff had standing because the intervenors "d[id] not claim that they ha[d] ever been threatened with prosecution, that a prosecution [wa]s likely, or even that a prosecution [was] remotely possible."

That is not this case. Unlike the intervenors in *Younger,* COAST has alleged an intent to engage in the same speech that was the subject of a prior enforcement proceeding. Also unlike the intervenors in *Younger,* who had never been threatened with prosecution, COAST has been the subject of Commission proceedings in the past. . . .

I. The Constitution and the Supreme Court

Page 107. Before section 3 of the Note, add the following:

The Court offered a new account of the foundations of the zone-of-interests test in Lexmark International v. Static Control Components, 134 S. Ct. 1377 (2014). Static Control Components contended that Lexmark had violated the Lanham Act by engaging in certain false and misleading conduct. In particular, Static Control Components claimed that Lexmark falsely advised companies that it was illegal to use Static Control's products to refurbish cartridges used for printing. Lexmark responded that courts should use "prudential standing" doctrines, and especially the zone-of-interests test, to deny standing to Static Control Components.

The Court unanimously disagreed. In an opinion by Justice Scalia, the Court said that the zone-of-interests test should be understood as posing an issue of statutory construction:

> Whether a plaintiff comes within "the 'zone of interests'" is an issue that requires us to determine, using traditional tools of statutory interpretation, whether a legislatively conferred cause of action encompasses a particular plaintiff's claim. As Judge Silberman of the D.C. Circuit recently observed, "'prudential standing' is a misnomer" as applied to the zone-of-interests analysis, which asks whether "this particular class of persons ha[s] a right to sue under this substantive statute." [In] sum, the question this case presents is whether Static Control falls within the class of plaintiffs whom Congress has authorized to sue under [the Lanham Act]. In other words, we ask whether Static Control has a cause of action under the statute. That question requires us to determine the meaning of the congressionally enacted provision creating a cause of action. In doing so, we apply traditional principles of statutory interpretation.

In a potentially important footnote, the Court added:

> The zone-of-interests test is not the only concept that we have previously classified as an aspect of "prudential standing" but for which, upon closer inspection, we have found that label inapt. Take, for example, our reluctance to entertain generalized grievances—i.e., suits "claiming only harm to [the plaintiff's] and every citizen's interest in proper application of the Constitution and laws, and seeking relief that no more directly and tangibly benefits him than it does the public at large." Lujan v. Defenders of Wildlife, 504 U.S. 555, 573-574 (1992). While we have at times grounded our reluctance to entertain such suits in the "counsels of prudence" (albeit counsels "close[ly] relat[ed] to the policies reflected in" Article III), Valley Forge Christian College v. Americans United for Separation of Church and

State, Inc., 454 U.S. 464, 475 (1982), we have since held that such suits do not present constitutional "cases" or "controversies." They are barred for constitutional reasons, not "prudential" ones.

(The problem of widely diffused harms is considered at page 110 of the main volume.)

On the merits, the Court concluded that Static Control did indeed have a right to sue, because the zone-of-interests test is "an appropriate tool for determining who may invoke the cause of action," because that test is not meant to be especially demanding, and because that "lenient approach is an appropriate means of preserving the flexibility of the APA's omnibus judicial-review provision, which permits suit for violations of numerous statutes of varying character that do not themselves include causes of action for judicial review." Under the Lanham Act, a plaintiff must allege an injury to a commercial interest in reputation or sales. Under that test, standing was available here:

> To begin, Static Control's alleged injuries—lost sales and damage to its business reputation—are injuries to precisely the sorts of commercial interests the Act protects. . . . There is no doubt that it is within the zone of interests protected by the statute.
>
> Static Control also sufficiently alleged that its injuries were proximately caused by Lexmark's misrepresentations. . . . [A]lthough diversion of sales to a direct competitor may be the paradigmatic direct injury from false advertising, it is not the only type of injury cognizable under [the Lanham Act].
>
> First, Static Control alleged that Lexmark disparaged its business and products by asserting that Static Control's business was illegal. When a defendant harms a plaintiff's reputation by casting aspersions on its business, the plaintiff's injury flows directly from the audience's belief in the disparaging statements. As we have observed, a defendant who "'seeks to promote his own interests by telling a known falsehood to or about the plaintiff or his product'" may be said to have proximately caused the plaintiff's harm.
>
> In addition, Static Control adequately alleged proximate causation by alleging that it designed, manufactured, and sold microchips that both (1) were necessary for, and (2) had no other use than, refurbishing Lexmark toner cartridges. . . . To invoke the Lanham Act's cause of action for false advertising, a plaintiff must plead (and ultimately prove) an injury to a commercial interest in sales or business reputation proximately caused by the defendant's misrepresentations. Static Control has adequately pleaded both elements.

Query: How, exactly, does the Court's formulation of the zone-of-interests test change preexisting law?

I. The Constitution and the Supreme Court

Page 118. At the end of the Note, add the following:

6. Perry *and* Windsor. The Court divided five-to-four on standing questions in two important cases involving same-sex marriage. The facts of United States v. Windsor, 133 S. Ct. 2675 (2013), were as follows. New York recognized the marriage of Edith Windsor and Thea Spyer, who wed in Ontario, Canada in 2007. Spyer died in 2009, leaving her estate to Windsor, who sought to claim the federal estate tax exemption for surviving spouses. She was barred from doing so by section 3 of the federal Defense of Marriage Act (DOMA), which defines "marriage" and "spouse" as excluding same-sex partners. Windsor paid $363,053 in estate taxes and sought a refund, which the Internal Revenue Service denied. Windsor brought suit, objecting that DOMA is inconsistent with the Fifth Amendment.

While the case was pending, the Attorney General notified the Speaker of the House of Representatives that the Department of Justice would no longer defend the constitutionality of section 3. In response, the Bipartisan Legal Advisory Group (BLAG) of the House of Representatives sought to intervene in the litigation to defend the constitutionality of section 3. The district court allowed intervention and ruled in Windsor's favor, ordering the Treasury to refund her tax with interest. The court of appeals affirmed. Although the United States agreed with the court's conclusion, it did not comply with the judgment, but instead sought certiorari in the Supreme Court.

In an opinion by Justice Kennedy (joined by Justices Breyer, Ginsburg, Sotomayor, and Kagan), the Court held that there was no standing problem:

> In this case the United States retains a stake sufficient to support Article III jurisdiction on appeal and in proceedings before this Court. The judgment in question orders the United States to pay Windsor the refund she seeks. An order directing the Treasury to pay money is "a real and immediate economic injury," indeed as real and immediate as an order directing an individual to pay a tax. That the Executive may welcome this order to pay the refund if it is accompanied by the constitutional ruling it wants does not eliminate the injury to the national Treasury if payment is made, or to the taxpayer if it is not. The judgment orders the United States to pay money that it would not disburse but for the court's order. The Government of the United States has a valid legal argument that it is injured even if the Executive disagrees with § 3 of DOMA, which results in Windsor's liability for the tax. Windsor's ongoing claim for funds that the United States refuses to pay thus establishes a controversy sufficient for Article III jurisdiction. It would be a different case if the Executive had taken the further step of paying Windsor the refund to which she was entitled under the District Court's ruling.

The Court acknowledged that "[a] party who receives all that he has sought generally is not aggrieved by the judgment affording the relief and cannot appeal from it." But it said that this rule "does not have its source in the jurisdictional limitations of Art. III. In an appropriate case, appeal may be permitted [at] the behest of the party who has prevailed on the merits, so long as that party retains a stake in the appeal satisfying the requirements of Art. III."

The Court also noted that there was a risk that the case lacked "concrete adversariness," because the executive branch was in agreement with Windsor. It concluded, however, that this problem involved not Article III but prudential considerations, and that those considerations were not sufficient to justify a refusal to rule on the merits:

> In the case now before the Court the attorneys for BLAG present a substantial argument for the constitutionality of § 3 of DOMA. BLAG's sharp adversarial presentation of the issues satisfies the prudential concerns that otherwise might counsel against hearing an appeal from a decision with which the principal parties agree. Were this Court to hold that prudential rules require it to dismiss the case, and, in consequence, that the Court of Appeals erred in failing to dismiss it as well, extensive litigation would ensue. The district courts in 94 districts throughout the Nation would be without precedential guidance not only in tax refund suits but also in cases involving the whole of DOMA's sweep involving over 1,000 federal statutes and a myriad of federal regulations. For instance, the opinion of the Court of Appeals for the First Circuit, addressing the validity of DOMA in a case involving regulations of the Department of Health and Human Services, likely would be vacated with instructions to dismiss, its ruling and guidance also then erased. Rights and privileges of hundreds of thousands of persons would be adversely affected, pending a case in which all prudential concerns about justiciability are absent. [In] these unusual and urgent circumstances, the very term "prudential" counsels that it is a proper exercise of the Court's responsibility to take jurisdiction. For these reasons, the prudential and Article III requirements are met here; and, as a consequence, the Court need not decide whether BLAG would have standing to challenge the District Court's ruling and its affirmance in the Court of Appeals on BLAG's own authority.

Justice Scalia (joined by Chief Justice Roberts and Justice Thomas) dissented. He wrote that "the plaintiff and the Government agree entirely on what should happen in this lawsuit. They agree that the court below got it right; and they agreed in the court below that the court below that one got it right as well. What, then, are we *doing* here?" He added:

I. The Constitution and the Supreme Court — Page 118

What the petitioner United States asks us to do in the case before us is exactly what the respondent Windsor asks us to do: not to provide relief from the judgment below but to say that that judgment was correct. And the same was true in the Court of Appeals: Neither party sought to undo the judgment for Windsor, and so that court should have dismissed the appeal (just as we should dismiss) for lack of jurisdiction. Since both parties agreed with the judgment of the District Court for the Southern District of New York, the suit should have ended there. The further proceedings have been a contrivance, having no object in mind except to elevate a District Court judgment that has no precedential effect in other courts, to one that has precedential effect throughout the Second Circuit, and then (in this Court) precedential effect throughout the United States.

In a separate dissenting opinion, Justice Alito essentially agreed with Justice Scalia with respect to the United States, but concluded that "the House of Representatives, which has authorized BLAG to represent its interests in this matter," suffered injury in fact, because the adverse decision had injured its ability to legislate. "In the narrow category of cases in which a court strikes down an Act of Congress and the Executive declines to defend the Act, Congress both has standing to defend the undefended statute and is a proper party to do so."

Having disposed of the standing issue, the Court reached the merits and held that DOMA was unconstitutional. This aspect of the case is considered in Chapter VI F 3 of this Supplement.

In Hollingsworth v. Perry, 133 S. Ct. 2652 (2013), the merits involved the constitutionality of a ballot initiative known as Proposition 8, which amended the California Constitution to define marriage as a union between a man and a woman. Same-sex couples, seeking to marry, filed suit in federal court, challenging Proposition 8 under the Fourteenth Amendment. After California officials (the named defendants) refused to defend the law, the district court allowed the initiative's official proponents to intervene to defend it. After a trial, the court declared Proposition 8 unconstitutional and enjoined public officials from enforcing it. Those officials elected not to appeal, but the proponents did so. The court of appeals certified to the California Supreme Court the question whether official proponents of a ballot initiative have authority to assert the State's interest in defending the constitutionality of the initiative when public officials refuse to do so. The California Supreme Court answered that they did.

Notwithstanding that answer, the Court concluded that the requirements of Article III were not met. Chief Justice Roberts (joined by Justices Scalia, Ginsburg, Breyer, and Kagan) explained that the proponents of the law had only a generalized grievance and no "direct stake" in the case. "Their only interest in having the District Court order reversed was to vindicate the constitutional validity of a generally applicable California law." To be sure, the proponents of a ballot proposition have a particular interest under California law, "but only when it comes to the process of enacting the law." After enactment, they "have no 'personal stake' in defending its enforcement that is distinguishable from the general interest of every citizen of California."

The Court acknowledged the proponents' argument that "even if they have no cognizable interest in appealing the District Court's judgment, the State of California does, and they may assert that interest on the State's behalf." But the Court responded that it is "a 'fundamental restriction on our authority' that '[i]n the ordinary course, a litigant must assert his or her own legal rights and interests, and cannot rest a claim to relief on the legal rights or interests of third parties.'" Exceptions to that presumption could not be found here. To the argument that California itself recognized a right here, the Court said that "no matter its reasons, the fact that a State thinks a private party should have standing to seek relief for a generalized grievance cannot override our settled law to the contrary. [We] have never before upheld the standing of a private party to defend the constitutionality of a state statute when state officials have chosen not to. We decline to do so for the first time here."

In dissent, Justice Kennedy (writing for himself and for Justices Thomas, Alito, and Sotomayor) emphasized that "[under] California law, a proponent has the authority to appear in court and assert the State's interest in defending an enacted initiative when the public officials charged with that duty refuse to do so." In his view, that authority is akin to a property right, one that gives rise to injury in fact. "Proponents' authority under state law is not a contrivance. It is not a fictional construct. It is the product of the California Constitution and the California Elections Code." As a matter of state law, the purpose of the initiative process "is undermined if the very officials the initiative process seeks to circumvent are the only parties who can defend an enacted initiative when it is challenged in a legal proceeding."

Is the Court's majority saying that a state lacks the constitutional power to create a legal right to defend the outcome of a referendum? If so, how is its decision consistent with *Akins*? Is *Windsor* consistent with *Perry*?

II
FEDERALISM AT WORK: CONGRESS AND THE NATIONAL ECONOMY

B. Doctrinal Fundamentals: Federalism and Judicial Review

Page 175. **At the end of section 2 of the Note, add the following:**

For a collection of essays whose general thrust is to update Wechsler's argument by drawing on more recent studies of the actual functioning of Congress, see Feature, Federalism as the New Nationalism, 123 Yale L.J. 1888 (2014).

C. The Evolution of the Commerce Clause Doctrine

Page 185. **After section 2 of the Note, add the following:**

2a. *Regulation or prohibition.* Consider the suggestion in Friedman & Lakier, "To Regulate," Not "To Prohibit": Limiting the Commerce Power, 2012 Sup. Ct. Rev. 255, 261-262 (2013):

> [In light of] Framing-era understandings of the proper division between the national and state government [and] modern economic analysis of the values of federalism, [the] only conceivable justification for allowing Congress to ban markets [is] to control the spillover costs of state diversity. [This] rationale standing alone is insufficient justification to allow Congress to prohibit commerce. [But Congress] would still be able to ban goods when

25

doing so serves [interstate] markets. [Because "in-service" laws do] not work to shut interstate commerce down, but instead typically help enforce rules by which interstate commerce operates, they do not represent prohibition of commerce. [Congress] would also have the power to adopt "helper" statutes [that] lend federal enforcement authority to states that have chosen through their own democratic processes to ban certain goods.

Page 199. At the end of section 4 of the Note, add the following:

The Chemical Weapons Convention Implementation Act prohibits the use of "any chemical weapon." The statute defines a chemical weapon as "[a] toxic chemical," and defines a toxic chemical as "any chemical which through its chemical action on life processes can cause death, temporary incapacitation or permanent harm to humans or animals. The term includes all such chemicals[.]" In Bond v. United States, 134 S. Ct. 2077 (2014), a defendant was prosecuted under the Act for spreading two chemicals on the car handles and mailbox of a woman who had become pregnant after intercourse with the defendant's husband. The chemicals "are toxic to humans and, in high enough doses, potentially lethal." The defendant challenged the constitutionality of the Act. Chief Justice Roberts for a six-person majority did not address the constitutional claims, but held that the Act did not apply to the defendant's actions. (For a discussion of the constitutional arguments, see page 30 of this Supplement, infra.) The majority "doubt[ed] that a treaty about *chemical weapons* has anything to do with Bond's conduct." The statute "must be read consistent with principles of [federalism]," which make it "appropriate to refer to basic principles of federalism [to] resolve ambiguity in a federal statute. In this case, the ambiguity derives from the improbably broad reach of the key statutory definition given the term — 'chemical weapon' — being defined; the deeply serious consequences of adopting such a boundless reading; and the lack of any apparent need to do so in light of the context from which the statute arose — a treaty about chemical warfare and terrorism." Justices Scalia, Thomas, and Alito each filed separate opinions concurring in the result. Each of them found that the statute covered the alleged conduct, but that it was unconstitutional.

Page 215. At the end of section 1 of the Note, add the following:

(In United States v. Windsor, 133 S. Ct. 2675 (2013), Justice Kennedy's opinion for the Court observed that the Defense of Marriage Act, held unconstitutional on equal protection grounds, was "an unusual deviation from the usual tradition of recognizing and accepting state definitions of marriage[, which] is strong evidence of a law having the purpose and effect of disapproval of that class." That "purpose and effect" were what rendered the statute unconstitutional as a violation of equality. *Windsor* is excerpted at greater length in Chapter VI F 3 of this Supplement.)

Page 217. At the end of section 4 of the Note, add the following:

For additional discussion of the necessary and proper clause, see United States v. Kebodeaux, 133 S. Ct. 2496 (2013).

Page 239. After section 5 of the Note, add the following:

6. *Why search for limits?* Rosen & Schmidt, Why Broccoli?: Limiting Principles and Popular Constitutionalism in the Health Care Case, 61 UCLA L. Rev. 66, 70, 71 (2013), argue that "a survey of constitutional history shows that when confronted with novel constitutional questions, the Court almost always declines to provide limiting principles that define the metes and bounds of the constitutional power or right at issue. Instead, [it] typically answers the question in a narrow [fashion] that analyzes [the] constitutionality of only the governmental action that is before the Court. Indeed, the Court typically avoids any attempt at identifying a limiting principle until it has considered the constitutional question many times, and not infrequently it declines to *ever* identify a limiting principle." Rosen and Schmidt connect the case to ideas about popular constitutionalism, and argue that the *NFIB* Court sought a limiting principle even though the constitutional question was novel because "popular constitutional demands [structured] public expectations about the stakes of the ACA challenge to such a degree that it would have been notable had the Court chosen not to go beyond the facts of the case to engage with the limits of congressional power."

For a collection of essays on *NFIB*, see Persilly, Metzger, & Morrison, eds., The Health Care Case: The Supreme Court's Decision and Its Implications (2013).

D. *State Regulation of Interstate Commerce*

Page 263. At the end of section 2 of the Note, add the following:

e. For a recent discussion of the privileges and immunities clause and the dormant commerce clause, see McBurney v. Young, 133 S. Ct. 1709 (2013), holding that a Virginia freedom of information statute limiting its use to state citizens is constitutional. According to the Court, statutory access to state-held information is not a "fundamental" right protected by the privileges and immunities clause, the distinction was not drawn to provide economic protection to citizens engaged in businesses using state-held information, and Virginia provided reasonable alternative methods by which out-of-state citizens could get access to information about judicial and other public proceedings. Questioning whether the statute triggered dormant commerce clause scrutiny (because the statute did not prohibit access to an interstate market or unduly burden such access), the Court held that the market-participant doctrine permitted the distinction because the state had created the market for information subject to the freedom of information act.

E. Preemption

Page 290. At the end of section 7 of the Note, add the following:

For an argument that *Arizona v. United States* exemplifies a distinctive form of "plenary power preemption," see Abrams, Plenary Power Preemption, 99 Va. L. Rev. 601 (2013). What subjects might be covered by such a doctrine, in addition to immigration/alienage and foreign affairs? In what sense is national power over such subjects "plenary" while national power over interstate commerce is not? How might "plenary power preemption" differ from "field preemption"?

III
THE SCOPE OF CONGRESS'S POWERS: TAXING AND SPENDING, WAR POWERS, INDIVIDUAL RIGHTS, AND STATE AUTONOMY

A. *Regulation Through Taxing, Spending, and the War Power*

Page 316. Replace "[The joint dissent concluded that the Medicaid expansion was inseverable from the Medicaid extension, and that the entire expansion, including the option for states to participate, therefore had to fall.]" with the following:

[The joint dissent concluded that the penalty for not participating in the Medicaid expansion was inseverable from the entire scheme of Medicaid expansion, and that the entire expansion, including the option for states to participate, therefore had to fall.]

Page 335   **III. Federalism At Work: Congress and the National Economy**

B. *Congress's Enforcement Powers under the Reconstruction Amendments*

Page 335. After section 3 of the Note, add the following:

3a. *Justifying "current burdens" by "current needs."* The Voting Rights Act of 1965 (VRA) adopted an aggressive remedy for protection of voting rights. Section 4 of the Act provided a "coverage formula" that singled out several states and political subdivisions that used literacy tests or similar devices as a prerequisite to voting and where registration or turnout in the 1964 election was significantly below the national average. The formula was amended in 1970 and 1975 to cover jurisdictions with low participation in either or both the 1968 or 1972 election. Those covered jurisdictions were required, under section 5 of the Act, to obtain federal approval before making changes in their voting laws. In 1982 and 2006, Congress extended section 5's "preclearance requirement" without changing the coverage formula.

In Shelby County v. Holder, 133 S. Ct. 2612 (2013), the Supreme Court, in an opinion by Chief Justice Roberts, held that the coverage formula of section 4 was unconstitutional and could no longer be used to subject jurisdictions to the preclearance regime of section 5.

Referring to its decision in Northwest Austin Municipal Utility District No. 1 v. Holder, 557 U.S. 193 (2009), the Court emphasized that "the Act imposes current burdens and must be justified by current needs." It saw the Act's preclearance regime as a departure from baseline constitutional principles because the Act "suspends 'all changes to state election law' — however innocuous — until they have been precleared by federal authorities in Washington, D.C.," requiring states to "beseech the Federal Government for permission to implement laws that they would otherwise have the right to enact and execute on their own," and because, "despite the tradition of equal sovereignty, the Act applies to only nine States (and several additional counties)." While "these departures from the basic features of our system of government" may have been justified by the pervasive discrimination that existed in 1965, they were no longer justified: "Nearly 50 years later, things have changed dramatically":

> When upholding the constitutionality of the coverage formula in 1966, we concluded that it was "rational in both practice and theory." The formula looked to cause (discriminatory tests) and effect (low voter registration and turnout), and tailored the remedy (preclearance) to those jurisdictions exhibiting both.
>
> By 2009, however, we concluded that the "coverage formula raise[d] serious constitutional questions." As we explained, a statute's "current

burdens" must be justified by "current needs," and any "disparate geographic coverage" must be "sufficiently related to the problem that it targets." The coverage formula met that test in 1965, but no longer does so.

Coverage today is based on decades-old data and eradicated practices. The formula captures States by reference to literacy tests and low voter registration and turnout in the 1960s and early 1970s. But such tests have been banned nationwide for over 40 years. And voter registration and turnout numbers in the covered States have risen dramatically in the years since. Racial disparity in those numbers was compelling evidence justifying the preclearance remedy and the coverage formula. There is no longer such a disparity.

In 1965, the States could be divided into two groups: those with a recent history of voting tests and low voter registration and turnout, and those without those characteristics. Congress based its coverage formula on that distinction. Today the Nation is no longer divided along those lines, yet the Voting Rights Act continues to treat it as if it were.

Justice Ginsburg, joined by Justices Breyer, Sotomayor, and Kagan, dissented. Their view was that Congress, rather than the Court, should decide whether the coverage formula remains appropriate:

It is well established that Congress' judgment regarding exercise of its power to enforce the Fourteenth and Fifteenth Amendments warrants substantial deference. The VRA addresses the combination of race discrimination and the right to vote, which is "preservative of all rights." Yick Wo v. Hopkins, 118 U.S. 356, 370 (1886). When confronting the most constitutionally invidious form of discrimination, and the most fundamental right in our democratic system, Congress' power to act is at its height.

The basis for this deference is firmly rooted in both constitutional text and precedent. The Fifteenth Amendment, which targets precisely and only racial discrimination in voting rights, states that, in this domain, "Congress shall have power to enforce this article by appropriate legislation." . . .

It cannot tenably be maintained that the VRA, an Act of Congress adopted to shield the right to vote from racial discrimination, is inconsistent with the letter or spirit of the Fifteenth Amendment, or any provision of the Constitution read in light of the Civil War Amendments. Nowhere in today's opinion [is] there clear recognition of the transformative effect the Fifteenth Amendment aimed to achieve. . . .

The stated purpose of the Civil War Amendments was to arm Congress with the power and authority to protect all persons within the Nation from violations of their rights by the States. In exercising that power, then, Congress may use "all means which are appropriate, which are plainly adapted" to the constitutional ends declared by these Amendments. McCulloch, 4 Wheat., at 421. So when Congress acts to enforce the right to vote free from racial discrimination, we ask not whether Congress has chosen the means most wise, but whether Congress has rationally selected means appropriate to a legitimate end. "It is not for us to review the congressional resolution of [the need for its chosen remedy]. It is enough that we be able to perceive a basis upon which the Congress might resolve the conflict as it did." Katzenbach v. Morgan, 384 U.S. 641, 653 (1966)....

For three reasons, legislation reauthorizing an existing statute is especially likely to satisfy the minimal requirements of the rational-basis test. First, when reauthorization is at issue, Congress has already assembled a legislative record justifying the initial legislation. Congress is entitled to consider that preexisting record as well as the record before it at the time of the vote on reauthorization....

Second, the very fact that reauthorization is necessary arises because Congress has built a temporal limitation into the Act....

Third, a reviewing court should expect the record supporting reauthorization to be less stark than the record originally made. Demand for a record of violations equivalent to the one earlier made would expose Congress to a catch-22. If the statute was working, there would be less evidence of discrimination, so opponents might argue that Congress should not be allowed to renew the statute. In contrast, if the statute was not working, there would be plenty of evidence of discrimination, but scant reason to renew a failed regulatory regime.

C. *The Tenth Amendment as a Federalism-Based Limitation on Congressional Power*

Page 348. After section 1 of the Note, add the following:

1a. *Constitutional limits on the power to implement treaties.* Bond v. United States, 134 S. Ct. 2077 (2014), involved a federal statute implementing the International Convention on the Prohibition of the Development, Production, Storage, Stockpiling, and Use of Chemical Weapons, a treaty ratified in 1997. A majority of the Court held that the statute did not apply to the defendant's actions. (See page 24 of this Supplement, supra.) Justice Scalia, concurring in the judgment, argued that the statute was unconstitutional because its only textual foundation was the necessary and proper clause. That clause gave Congress the power to

III. Federalism At Work: Congress and the National Economy

make laws necessary and proper for carrying into execution" the "Power [to] make Treaties." It did not grant to Congress a "power to execute the treaties themselves." It gave Congress the power to "appropriate[ ] money for hiring treaty negotiators, [or to pay] for a bevy of spies to monitor the treaty-related deliberations of other potential signatories. [A] power to help the President *make* treaties is not a power to *implement* treaties already made. [To] legislate compliance with the United States' treaty obligations, Congress must rely upon its independent [Article] I, §8, powers." Justice Thomas joined this part of Justice Scalia's opinion.

Justice Thomas, joined by Justice Scalia and in substantial part by Justice Alito, also concurred in the result, "suggest[ing] that the Treaty Power is [a] limited federal power," which "can be used to arrange intercourse with other nations, but not to regulate purely domestic affairs." He did not offer a definition of "intercourse with other nations," but used the term to refer to treaties "dealing with conditions of commerce, with mutual defense, with belligerent relations, with rights of passage [etc.]." He quoted Madison: "The Federal Government's powers ['will'] be exercised principally on external objects, as war, peace, negotiation, and foreign commerce—the traditional subjects of treaty-making." He acknowledged that "the Federal Government needed the ability to respond to unforeseeable varieties of intercourse with other nations," but, again quoting Madison, any exercise of the Treaty Power "'must be consistent with the object of the delegation,' which is 'the regulation of intercourse with foreign nations.'"

IV
THE DISTRIBUTION OF NATIONAL POWERS

C. Foreign Affairs

Page 389. At the end of section 2 of the Note, add the following:

Consider also Bradley & Morrison, Historical Gloss and the Separation of Powers, 126 Harv. L. Rev. 411, 414-415 (2012):

[The] concept of institutional acquiescence needs to be tied more closely to the reality of how the political branches actually interact. Claims about acquiescence are typically based on a Madisonian conception of interbranch competition pursuant to which Congress and the Executive are each assumed to have the tools and motivation to guard against encroachments on their authority. It has become apparent from political science scholarship, however, that the Madisonian model does not accurately reflect the dynamics of modern congressional-executive relations. [Although] Congress and the President may disagree about particular policies, Congress as a body does not systematically seek to protect its prerogatives against presidential encroachment.

Bradley and Morrison conclude that this fact argues "not so much for rejecting the idea of acquiescence altogether as for being more cautious about treating apparently legislative inaction as acquiescence, and for looking beyond formal enactments when assessing whether any given case actually involves acquiescence or nonacquiescence." In particular, a finding of acquiescence may be more defensible "when the practice in question is not only long standing but also the product of bipartisan choices." Id.

D. Domestic Affairs

Page 423. After the first paragraph of section 3 of the Note, add the following:

For a discussion of the extent to which, and methods by which, the president is controlled by law rather than politics, see Bradley & Morrison, Presidential Power, Historical Practice, and Legal Constraint, 113 Colum. L. Rev. 1097 (2013). For arguments that legal constraints on the executive have mostly collapsed, see B. Ackerman, The Decline and Fall of the American Republic (2010); E. Posner & A. Vermeule, The Executive Unbound: After the Madisonian Republic (2010).

Page 435. At the end of section 1 of the Note, add the following:

Consider the "Regulation from the Executive in Need of Scrutiny Act of 2011," passed by the House of Representatives in 2011, REINS Act, H.R. 10, 112th Cong., § 3, which provides that a "major rule [promulgated by an administrative agency] shall not take effect unless the Congress enacts a joint resolution of approval." The Senate has not passed the Act. If it were enacted into law, would it be constitutional? Compare Statement of Rep. John Conyers, Jr., Ranking Member, H. Comm. on the Judiciary, REINS Act—Promoting Jobs and Expanding Freedom by Reducing Needless Regulations: Hearings Before the Subcomm. on Courts, Commercial & Admin. Law of the H. Comm. on the Judiciary, 112th Cong. 8 (2011) (arguing that the Act would violate *Chadha* because if an agency promulgated a rule, either House of Congress acting alone could block it by not passing a resolution of approval), with Siegel, The REINS Act and the Struggle to Control Agency Rulemaking, 16 N.Y.U. J. Legis. & Pub. Pol'y 131, 185 (2013) (arguing that the Act is "a bad idea" because Congress lacks the time and expertise to decide these questions but that it is "perfectly constitutional" because it "merely reclaim[s] the power that Congress has ceded over time").

Page 451. After section 4 of the Note, add the following:

4a. *Recess appointments.* Article II, section 2, clause 2 of the Constitution requires the advice and consent of the Senate for most presidential appointments, but Article II, section 2, clause 3 provides that "[the] President shall have the Power to fill up all Vacancies that may happen during the Recess of the Senate,

IV. The Distribution of National Powers

by granting Commissions which shall expire at the End of [Congress's] next session. In National Labor Relations Board v. Noel Canning, 34 S. Ct. 2550 (2014), the Supreme Court for the first time adjudicated a case concerning the scope of this power.

The case arose amidst intense political controversy over the use of the Senate filibuster to block presidential appointments (sometimes because of opposition to the existence of the agency in question rather than because of opposition to the particular nominee) and over the President's attempt to circumvent filibusters by making recess appointments. When the Senate delayed the confirmation of three members of the National Labor Relations Board, President Obama used his recess appointments power to place them on the Board. He made the appointments after the Senate adopted a resolution providing that it would take a series of brief recesses beginning on December 17, 2011. The resolution provided that the Senate would hold "pro forma" sessions every Tuesday and Friday until it returned to ordinary business on January 23, 2012. President Obama made the appointments on January 4, between the January 3 and January 6 pro forma sessions.

Noel Canning, which had been found by the Board to have violated the labor laws, claimed that the Board lacked a quorum to act because three of the Board's five members had been illegally appointed.

The Court of Appeals agreed with Noel Canning that the appointments were illegal because, in its view, the words "the recess of the Senate" referred only to Congress's annual inter-session recess, not to its more frequent intra-session recesses, and because the words "vacancies that may happen during the recess" referred only to vacancies that come into existence during the recess, not to vacancies that occur earlier but that remain unfilled during a recess.

By a vote of five to four, the Court, per Justice Breyer, rejected both of these arguments. It nonetheless held that the appointments were illegal. The Court reasoned that the *pro forma* sessions brought to a close the recesses between them. This meant that the appointments occurred during a three-day recess, and the Court held that a "recess of [less] than 10 days is presumptively too short to fall within the Clause. We add the word 'presumptively' to leave open the possibility that some very unusual circumstance—a national catastrophe, for instance, that renders the Senate unavailable but calls for an urgent response—could demand the exercise of the recess-appointment power during a shorter break."

In reaching these conclusions, the Court emphasized its view that the recess appointments power was not meant to "[offer] the President the authority routinely to avoid the need for Senate confirmation." It also emphasized the role of historical practice in interpreting the scope of the power. "We recognize, of course, that the separation of powers can serve to safeguard individual liberty and that it is the 'duty of the judicial department'—in a separation-of-power case as in any other—'to say what the law is' [quoting Marbury v. Madison]. But it is equally true that the longstanding 'practice of government' [quoting McCulloch

v. Maryland] can inform our determination of 'what the law is.'" With regard to the second point, the Court noted that

> Presidents have made recess appointments since the beginning of the Republic. Their frequency suggests that the Senate and President have recognized that recess appointments can be both necessary and appropriate in certain circumstances. We have not previously interpreted the Clause, and, when doing so for the first time in more than 200 years, we must hesitate to upset the compromises and working arrangements that the elected branches of Government themselves have reached.

The Court then turned its attention to whether the clause permitted intra-session as well as inter-session recesses. Finding the term "the recess" ambiguous, the Court relied on its purpose, which, it held, "[demands] the broader interpretation" because "[the] Senate is equally away during both an inter-session and an intra-session recess, and its capacity to participate in the appointments process has nothing to do with the words it uses to signal its departure." In addition, the Court cited a record of frequent intra-session appointments from the post–Civil War period to the present and opinions by the President's legal advisors supporting these appointments.

> The upshot is that restricting the Clause to inter-session recesses would frustrate its purpose. It would make the President's recess-appointment power dependent on a formalistic distinction of Senate procedure. Moreover, the President has consistently and frequently interpreted the word "recess" to apply to intra-session recesses, and has acted on that interpretation. The Senate as a body has done nothing to deny the validity of this practice for at least three-quarters of a century. And three-quarters of a century of settled practice is long enough to entitle a practice to "great weight in a proper interpretation of the constitutional provision."

The Court then considered the second ground on which the lower court had invalidated the appointment—that the vacancy had not "happened" during the recess because it did not initially occur while the Senate was in recess. Once again, the Court found that the language itself was ambiguous, but that its purpose suggested a broader interpretation. The Court reasoned that the President might not have time to fill a vacancy before the Senate went into recess and that, if the office was an important one, the inability to fill the post while the Senate was not in session could have serious adverse consequences. The Court again found that historical practice for more than 200 years supported this interpretation. While recognizing that the interpretation might be thought to allow the President to routinely avoid the confirmation process by making all appointments during

IV. The Distribution of National Powers   Page 451

recesses, the Court pointed out that this course of conduct had disadvantages, including the fact that the appointee can only serve for a limited term and her provisional status might make her less effective. "Moreover, the Senate, like the President, has institutional 'resources,' including political resources 'available to protect and assert its interests.'"

Finally, the Court turned to the issue of how to treat the "pro forma" sessions. The government argued that these sessions were periods of recess because the Senate did virtually no business during them and was therefore in recess as a functional matter. The Court disagreed:

> [The] Senate is in session when it says it is, provided that, under its own rules, it retains the capacity to transact Senate business. The Senate met that standard here.
>
> The standard we apply is consistent with the Constitution's broad delegation of authority to the Senate to determine how and when to conduct its business. The Constitution explicitly empowers the Senate to "determine the Rules of its Proceedings." Art. I, § 5, cl. 2. . . .
>
> In addition the Constitution provides the Senate with extensive control over its schedule. . . .
>
> We generally take at face value the Senate's own report of its actions.

Since pro forma sessions interrupted the recess, the Court was forced to decide whether the period between these sessions was long enough to trigger the recess appointments power. It concluded that it was not:

> The Recess Appointments Clause seeks to permit the Executive Branch to function smoothly when Congress is unavailable. And though Congress has taken short breaks for almost 200 years, and there have been many thousands of recess appointments in that time, we have not found a single example of a recess appointment made during an intra-session recess that was shorter than 10 days. . . . The lack of examples suggests that the recess appointment power is not needed in that context.

Justice Scalia, in an opinion joined by Chief Justice Roberts and Justices Thomas and Alito, concurred in the judgment. He would have held that the recess appointments power arises only during the annual intermission between two formal legislative sessions and that the recess must first occur during that period. He accused the majority of justifying its "atextual results on an adverse-possession theory of executive authority." In Justice Scalia's view,

> The Court's decision transforms the recess-appointment power from a tool carefully designed to fill a narrow and specific need into a weapon to be

wielded by future Presidents against future Senates. To reach that result, the majority casts aside the plain original meaning of the constitutional text in deference to late-arising historical practices that are ambiguous at best. The majority's insistence on deferring to the Executive's untenably broad interpretation of the power is in clear conflict with our precedent and forebodes a diminution of this Court's role in controversies involving the separation of powers and the structure of government.

Justice Scalia emphasized that because "separation of power exists for the protection of individual liberty," it was irrelevant that the Senate had approved of or not objected to the encroachment. "Plainly . . . a self-aggrandizing practice adopted by one branch well after the founding, often challenged, and never before blessed by this Court . . . does not relieve us of our duty to interpret the Constitution in light of its text, structure, and original understanding."

Moreover, Justice Scalia's review of the historical record convinced him that prior practice was "at best ambiguous."

> Even if the Executive could accumulate power through adverse possession by engaging in a *consistent* and *unchallenged* practice over a long period of time, the oft-disputed practices at issue here would not meet that standard. Nor have those practices created any justifiable expectations that could be disappointed by enforcing the Constitution's original meaning. . . .
>
> The real tragedy of today's decision is not simply the abolition of the Constitution's limits on the recess-appointment power and the substitution of a novel framework invented by this Court. It is the damage done to our separation-of-powers jurisprudence more generally. [We] should [take] every opportunity to affirm the primacy of the Constitution's enduring principles over the politics of the moment. Our failure to do so today will resonate well beyond the particular dispute at hand. Sad, but true: The Court's embrace of the adverse-possession theory of executive power [will] be cited in diverse contexts, including those presently unimagined, and will have the effect of aggrandizing the Presidency beyond its constitutional bounds and undermining respect for the separation of powers.

V
EQUALITY AND THE CONSTITUTION

C. *Equal Protection Methodology: Heightened Scrutiny and the Problem of Race*

Page 598. At the end of the page, add the following:

Are there methods of achieving the goals of affirmative action without utilizing facially racial classifications? Consider S. Cashin, Place not Race: A New Vision of Opportunity in America at xix (2014):

> The rub for proponents of affirmative action is that as long as they hold on to race as the sine qua non of diversity, they stymie possibilities for transformative change. The civil rights community, for example, expends energy on a policy that primarily benefits the most advantaged children of color, while contributing to a divisive politics that makes it difficult to create quality K-12 education for all children. [The] next generation of diversity strategies should encourage rather than discourage cross-racial alliances and social mobility. [Meaningful] diversity can be achieved if institutions rethink exclusionary practices, cultivate strivers from overlooked places, and give special consideration to highly qualified applicants of all races that have had to overcome structural disadvantages like segregation.

Has the Supreme Court tightened up the narrow tailoring requirement announced in *Grutter*? Consider the following:

FISHER v. UNIVERSITY OF TEXAS, 133 S. Ct. 2411 (2013). After the Fifth Circuit held in Hopwood v. Texas, 78 F.3d 932 (1996), that the University of Texas's consideration of race in its admissions process violated the equal protection clause because it did not further a compelling government interest, the Texas legislature adopted a measure known as the Top Ten Percent Law. That statute granted automatic admission to the University (as well as other public institutions) to all students from Texas high schools who are in the top 10 percent of their class. Following the Supreme Court's decision in Grutter v. Bollinger, 539 U.S. 306 (2003), holding that racial diversity can be a compelling government interest, the University adopted an additional admissions program in which race was one factor taken into account in admitting the portion of the entering class that was not admitted under the Top Ten Percent Law.

Alison Fisher, a white student who had been denied admission to the University, brought suit, alleging that the University's consideration of race violated the equal protection clause. The district court and the court of appeals ruled in favor of the University, holding that the University was entitled to substantial deference both in deciding that racial diversity was a compelling state interest and in deciding how to achieve that diversity.

The Supreme Court, in an opinion by Justice Kennedy, reversed, holding that the court of appeals had not applied "the correct standard of strict scrutiny." The Court took as given its prior decisions in Regents of University of California v. Bakke, 438 U.S. 265 (1978); *Grutter*; and Gratz v. Bollinger, 539 U.S. 244 (2003), which had found that "the interest in the educational benefits that flow from a diverse student body" was "one compelling interest that could justify the consideration of race."

"Once the University has established that its goal of diversity is consistent with strict scrutiny, however, there must still be a further judicial determination that the admissions process meets strict scrutiny in its implementation. The University must prove that the means chosen by the University to attain diversity are narrowly tailored to that goal. On this point, the University receives no deference. *Grutter* made clear that it is for the courts, not for university administrators, to ensure that '[t]he means chosen to accomplish the [government's] asserted purpose must be specifically and narrowly framed to accomplish that purpose.' True, a court can take account of a university's experience and expertise in adopting or rejecting certain admissions processes. But, as the Court said in *Grutter*, it remains at all times the University's obligation to demonstrate, and the Judiciary's obligation to determine, that admissions processes 'ensure that each applicant is evaluated as an individual and not in a way that makes an applicant's race or ethnicity the defining feature of his or her application.'

"Narrow tailoring also requires that the reviewing court verify that it is 'necessary' for a university to use race to achieve the educational benefits of diversity. *Bakke*. This involves a careful judicial inquiry into whether a university could achieve sufficient diversity without using racial classifications. Although '[n]arrow tailoring does not require exhaustion of every conceivable race-neutral alternative,' strict scrutiny does require a court to examine with care, and not defer to, a university's 'serious, good faith consideration of workable race-neutral alternatives.' See *Grutter*. Consideration by the university is of course necessary, but it

V. Equality and the Constitution   Page 598

is not sufficient to satisfy strict scrutiny: The reviewing court must ultimately be satisfied that no workable race-neutral alternatives would produce the educational benefits of diversity. If '"a nonracial approach . . . could promote the substantial interest about as well and at tolerable administrative expense,"' Wygant v. Jackson Bd. of Ed., 476 U.S. 267, 280, n.6 (1986) (quoting Greenawalt, Judicial Scrutiny of "Benign" Racial Preference in Law School Admissions, 75 Colum. L. Rev. 559, 578-579 (1975)), then the university may not consider race. A plaintiff, of course, bears the burden of placing the validity of a university's adoption of an affirmative action plan in issue. But strict scrutiny imposes on the university the ultimate burden of demonstrating, before turning to racial classifications, that available, workable race-neutral alternatives do not suffice."

Because the court of appeals had instead presumed that the University's decision to reintroduce race as an admissions factor was permissible, the Supreme Court remanded the case "so that the admissions process can be considered and judged under a correct analysis."

Justice Scalia wrote a short concurring opinion adhering to the view he expressed in *Grutter* that the Fourteenth Amendment "proscribes government discrimination on the basis of race, and state-provided education is no exception," but noting that because Fisher had not asked the Court to overrule *Grutter*, he joined the Court's opinion.

Justice Thomas wrote a lengthier concurrence, taking the position that "a State's use of race in higher education admissions decisions is categorically prohibited by the Equal Protection Clause." He saw "nothing 'pressing' or 'necessary' about obtaining whatever educational benefits may flow from racial diversity":

"[T]he educational benefits flowing from student body diversity—assuming they exist—hardly qualify as a compelling state interest. Indeed, the argument that educational benefits justify racial discrimination was advanced in support of racial segregation in the 1950's, but emphatically rejected by this Court. And just as the alleged educational benefits of segregation were insufficient to justify racial discrimination then, see Brown v. Board of Education, 347 U.S. 483 (1954), the alleged educational benefits of diversity cannot justify racial discrimination today."

He then drew a series of parallels between the arguments advanced by the University and the arguments that had been advanced in favor of racial segregation:

"The University asserts, for instance, that the diversity obtained through its discriminatory admissions program prepares its students to become leaders in a diverse society. See, e.g., Brief for Respondents 6 (arguing that student body diversity 'prepares students to become the next generation of leaders in an increasingly diverse society'). The segregationists likewise defended segregation on the ground that it provided more leadership opportunities for blacks. See, e.g., Brief for Respondents in Sweatt 96 ('[A] very large group of Northern Negroes [comes] South to attend separate colleges, suggesting that the Negro does not secure as well-rounded a college life at a mixed college, and that the separate college offers him positive advantages; that there is a more normal social life for the Negro in a separate college; that there is a greater opportunity for full participation and for the development of leadership; that the Negro is inwardly more "secure" at a college of his own people'); Brief for Appellees in Davis 25-26 ('The Negro child gets an opportunity to participate in segregated schools that I have never seen accorded to him in non-segregated schools. He is important, he holds offices, he is accepted by his fellows, he is on athletic teams, he has a full place there' (internal quotation marks omitted)). This argument was unavailing. It is irrelevant under the Fourteenth Amendment whether segregated or mixed schools produce better leaders. Indeed, no court today would accept the suggestion that segregation is permissible because historically black colleges produced Booker T. Washington, Thurgood Marshall, Martin Luther King, Jr., and other prominent leaders. Likewise, the University's racial discrimination cannot be justified on the ground that it will produce better leaders.

"The University also asserts that student body diversity improves interracial relations. See, e.g., Brief for Respondents 6 (arguing that student body diversity promotes 'cross-racial understanding' and breaks down racial and ethnic stereotypes). In this argument, too, the University repeats arguments once marshaled in support of segregation. See, e.g., Brief for Appellees in Davis 17 ('Virginia has established segregation in certain fields as a part of her public policy to prevent violence and reduce resentment. The result, in the view of an overwhelming Virginia majority, has been to improve the relationship between the different races'); id., at 25 ('If segregation be stricken down, the general welfare will be definitely harmed . . . there would be more friction developed' (internal quotation marks omitted)); Brief for Respondents in Sweatt 93 ('Texas has had no serious breaches of the peace in recent years in connection with its schools. The separation of the races has kept the conflicts at a minimum'); id., at 97-98 ('The legislative acts are based not only on the belief that it is the best way to provide education for both races, and the knowledge that separate schools are necessary to keep public support for the public schools, but upon the necessity to maintain the public peace, harmony, and welfare'); Brief for Appellees in Briggs 32 ('The southern Negro, by and large, does not want an end to segregation in itself any more than does the southern white man. The Negro in the South knows that discriminations, and worse, can and would multiply in such event' (internal quotation marks omitted)). We flatly rejected this line of arguments in McLaurin v. Oklahoma State Regents for Higher Ed., 339 U.S. 637 (1950), where we held that segregation would be unconstitutional even if white students never tolerated blacks. Id., at 641 ('It may be argued that appellant will be in no better position when these restrictions are removed, for he may still be set apart by his fellow students. This we think irrelevant.

V. Equality and the Constitution   Page 598

There is a vast difference—a Constitutional difference—between restrictions imposed by the state which prohibit the intellectual commingling of students, and the refusal of individuals to commingle where the state presents no such bar'). It is, thus, entirely irrelevant whether the University's racial discrimination increases or decreases tolerance.

"Finally, while the University admits that racial discrimination in admissions is not ideal, it asserts that it is a temporary necessity because of the enduring race consciousness of our society. See Brief for Respondents 53-54 ('Certainly all aspire for a colorblind society in which race does not matter. . . . But in Texas, as in America, "our highest aspirations are yet unfulfilled"'). Yet again, the University echoes the hollow justifications advanced by the segregationists. See, e.g., Brief for State of Kansas on Reargument in Brown v. Board of Education, O.T. 1953, No. 1, p. 56 ('We grant that segregation may not be the ethical or political ideal. At the same time we recognize that practical considerations may prevent realization of the ideal'); Brief for Respondents in Sweatt 94 ('The racial consciousness and feeling which exists today in the minds of many people may be regrettable and unjustified. Yet they are a reality which must be dealt with by the State if it is to preserve harmony and peace and at the same time furnish equal education to both groups'); id., at 96 ('"[T]he mores of racial relationships are such as to rule out, for the present at least, any possibility of admitting white persons and Negroes to the same institutions"'); Brief for Appellees in Briggs 26-27 ('[I]t would be unwise in administrative practice . . . to mix the two races in the same schools at the present time and under present conditions'); Brief for Appellees on Reargument in Briggs v. Elliott, O.T. 1953, No. 2, p. 79 ('It is not "racism" to be cognizant of the fact that mankind has struggled with race problems and racial tensions for upwards of sixty centuries'). But these arguments too were unavailing. The Fourteenth Amendment views racial bigotry as an evil to be stamped out, not as an excuse for perpetual racial tinkering by the State. See DeFunis v. Odegaard, 416 U.S. 312, 342 (1974) (Douglas, J., dissenting) ('The Equal Protection Clause commands the elimination of racial barriers, not their creation in order to satisfy our theory as to how society ought to be organized'). The University's arguments to this effect are similarly insufficient to justify discrimination. . . .

"The worst forms of racial discrimination in this Nation have always been accompanied by straight-faced representations that discrimination helped minorities.

"Slaveholders argued that slavery was a 'positive good' that civilized blacks and elevated them in every dimension of life. . . .

"A century later, segregationists similarly asserted that segregation was not only benign, but good for black students. They argued, for example, that separate schools protected black children from racist white students and teachers. . . .

"Following in these inauspicious footsteps, the University would have us believe that its discrimination is likewise benign. I think the lesson of history is clear enough: Racial discrimination is never benign. . . .

"While it does not, for constitutional purposes, matter whether the University's racial discrimination is benign, I note that racial engineering does in fact have insidious consequences. There can be no doubt that the University's discrimination injures white and Asian applicants who are denied admission because of their race. But I believe the injury to those admitted under the University's discriminatory admissions program is even more harmful.

"Blacks and Hispanics admitted to the University as a result of racial discrimination are, on average, far less prepared than their white and Asian classmates. In the University's entering class of 2009, for example, among the students admitted outside the Top Ten Percent plan, blacks scored at the 52d percentile of 2009 SAT takers nationwide, while Asians scored at the 93d percentile. Blacks had a mean GPA of 2.57 and a mean SAT score of 1524; Hispanics had a mean GPA of 2.83 and a mean SAT score of 1794; whites had a mean GPA of 3.04 and a mean SAT score of 1914; and Asians had a mean GPA of 3.07 and a mean SAT score of 1991. . . .

"The University admits minorities who otherwise would have attended less selective colleges where they would have been more evenly matched. But, as a result of the mismatching, many blacks and Hispanics who likely would have excelled at less elite schools are placed in a position where underperformance is all but inevitable because they are less academically prepared than the white and Asian students with whom they must compete. Setting aside the damage wreaked upon the self-confidence of these overmatched students, there is no evidence that they learn more at the University than they would have learned at other schools for which they were better prepared. Indeed, they may learn less. . . .

"[T]hese students may well drift towards less competitive majors because the mismatch caused by racial discrimination in admissions makes it difficult for them to compete in more rigorous majors.

"Moreover, the University's discrimination 'stamp[s] [blacks and Hispanics] with a badge of inferiority.' *Adarand*, 515 U.S., at 241 (opinion of Thomas, J.). It taints the accomplishments of all those who are admitted as a result of racial discrimination. Cf. J. McWhorter, Losing the Race: Self-Sabotage in Black America 248 (2000) ('I was never able to be as proud of getting into Stanford as my classmates could be. . . . [H]ow much of an achievement can I truly say it was to have been a good enough black person to be admitted, while my colleagues had been considered good enough people to be admitted'). And, it taints the accomplishments of all those who are the same race as those admitted as a result of racial discrimination. In this case, for example, most blacks and Hispanics attending the

V. Equality and the Constitution   Page 612

University were admitted without discrimination under the Top Ten Percent plan, but no one can distinguish those students from the ones whose race played a role in their admission. . . ."

Justice Ginsburg issued a short dissent, stating that she would have upheld the University's admissions policy:

"Petitioner urges that Texas' Top Ten Percent Law and race-blind holistic review of each application achieve significant diversity, so the University must be content with those alternatives. I have said before and reiterate here that only an ostrich could regard the supposedly neutral alternatives as race unconscious. See *Gratz*, 539 U.S., at 303-304, n.10 (dissenting opinion). As Justice Souter observed, the vaunted alternatives suffer from 'the disadvantage of deliberate obfuscation.' Id., at 297-298 (dissenting opinion).

"Texas' percentage plan was adopted with racially segregated neighborhoods and schools front and center stage. . . ." In a footnote, she added that "[t]he notion that Texas' Top Ten Percent Law is race neutral calls to mind Professor Thomas Reed Powell's famous statement: 'If you think that you can think about a thing inextricably attached to something else without thinking of the thing which it is attached to, then you have a legal mind.' T. Arnold, The Symbols of Government 101 (1935) (internal quotation marks omitted). Only that kind of legal mind could conclude that an admissions plan specifically designed to produce racial diversity is not race conscious."

"Among constitutionally permissible options, I remain convinced, 'those that candidly disclose their consideration of race [are] preferable to those that conceal it.' *Gratz*, 539 U.S., at 305, n.11 (dissenting opinion).

"Accordingly, I would not return this case for a second look. . . ."

Justice Kagan did not participate.

Page 612. At the conclusion of Chief Justice Roberts's opinion, add the following paragraph:

Before *Brown*, schoolchildren were told where they could and could not go to school based on the color of their skin. The school districts in these cases have not carried the heavy burden of demonstrating that we should allow this once again—even for very different reasons. For schools that never segregated on the basis of race, such as Seattle, or that have removed the vestiges of past segregation, such as Jefferson County, the way "to achieve a system of determining admission to the public schools on a nonracial basis," *Brown II*, is to stop assigning students on a racial basis. The way to stop discrimination on the basis of race is to stop discriminating on the basis of race.

Page 624. Before the Note, add the following:

SCHUETTE v. COALITION TO DEFEND AFFIRMATIVE ACTION, INTEGRATION & IMMIGRANT RIGHTS & FIGHT FOR EQUALITY BY ANY MEANS NECESSARY (BAMN)

134 S. Ct. 1623 (2014)

JUSTICE KENNEDY announced the judgment of the Court and delivered an opinion, in which [CHIEF JUSTICE ROBERTS] and JUSTICE ALITO join.

[In 2006, after the Court's decisions in *Gratz* and *Grutter*, voters of Michigan adopted Proposal 2, which amended Michigan's constitution by adding Article I, section 26. The amendment provided as follows:

[(1) The University of Michigan, Michigan State University, Wayne State University, and any other public college or university, community college, or school district shall not discriminate against, or grant preferential treatment to, any individual or group on the basis of race, sex, color, ethnicity, or national origin in the operation of public employment, public education, or public contracting.

[(2) The state shall not discriminate against, or grant preferential treatment to, any individual or group on the basis of race, sex, color, ethnicity, or national origin in the operation of public employment, public education, or public contracting.

[(3) For the purposes of this section 'state' includes, but is not necessarily limited to, the state itself, any city, county, any public college, university, or community college, school district, or other political subdivision or governmental instrumentality of or within the State of Michigan not included in sub-section 1.

[The District Court rejected an equal protection challenge to the amendment, but the Court of Appeals reversed.]

Before the Court addresses the question presented, it is important to note what this case is not about. It is not about the constitutionality, or the merits, of race-conscious admissions policies in higher education. [The] question here concerns not the permissibility of race-conscious admissions policies under the Constitution but whether, and in what manner, voters in the States may choose to prohibit the consideration of racial preferences in governmental decisions, in particular with respect to school admissions.

V. Equality and the Constitution

This Court has noted that some States have decided to prohibit race-conscious admissions policies. In *Grutter,* the Court noted: "Universities in California, Florida, and Washington State, where racial preferences in admissions are prohibited by state law, are currently engaged in experimenting with a wide variety of alternative approaches. Universities in other States can and should draw on the most promising aspects of these race-neutral alternatives as they develop." In this way, *Grutter* acknowledged the significance of a dialogue regarding this contested and complex policy question among and within States. . . .

[This] Court's decision in Reitman v. Mulkey, 387 U.S. 369 (1967), is a proper beginning point for discussing the controlling decisions. [*Mulkey* is discussed at page 1570 of the main volume.] In *Mulkey,* voters amended the California Constitution to prohibit any state legislative interference with an owner's prerogative to decline to sell or rent residential property on any basis. [The] Court agreed with the California Supreme Court that the amendment operated to insinuate the State into the decision to discriminate by encouraging that practice. The Court noted the "immediate design and intent" of the amendment was to "establis[h] a purported constitutional right to privately discriminate." The Court agreed that the amendment "expressly authorized and constitutionalized the private right to discriminate." The effect of the state constitutional amendment was to "significantly encourage and involve the State in private racial discriminations." . . .

The next precedent of relevance, Hunter v. Erickson, 393 U.S. 385 (1969), is central to the arguments the respondents make in the instant case. [*Hunter* is discussed at page 537 of the main volume.] In *Hunter,* the Court for the first time elaborated what the Court of Appeals here styled the "political process" doctrine. There, the Akron City Council found that the citizens of Akron consisted of "'people of different race[s], . . . many of whom live in circumscribed and segregated areas, under sub-standard unhealthful, unsafe, unsanitary and overcrowded conditions, because of discrimination in the sale, lease, rental and financing of housing.'" To address the problem, Akron enacted a fair housing ordinance to prohibit that sort of discrimination. In response, voters amended the city charter to overturn the ordinance and to require that any additional antidiscrimination housing ordinance be approved by referendum. But most other ordinances "regulating the real property market" were not subject to those threshold requirements. . . .

Central to the Court's reasoning in *Hunter* was that the charter amendment was enacted in circumstances where widespread racial discrimination in the sale and rental of housing led to segregated housing, forcing many to live in "'unhealthful, unsafe, unsanitary and overcrowded conditions.'" [The] Court found that the city charter amendment, by singling out antidiscrimination ordinances, "places special burden on racial minorities within the governmental process," thus becoming as impermissible as any other government action taken with the invidious intent to injure a racial minority. [*Hunter*] rests on the unremarkable principle that the State may not alter the procedures of government to target racial minorities. The facts in *Hunter* established that invidious discrimination would be the necessary result of the procedural restructuring. Thus, in *Mulkey* and *Hunter*, there was a demonstrated injury on the basis of race that, by reasons of state encouragement or participation, became more aggravated.

[Washington v. Seattle School District No. 1, 458 U.S. 457 (1982),] is the third case of principal relevance here. There, the school board adopted a mandatory busing program to alleviate racial isolation of minority students in local schools. Voters who opposed the school board's busing plan passed a state initiative that barred busing to desegregate. The Court first determined that, although "white as well as Negro children benefit from" diversity, the school board's plan "inures primarily to the benefit of the minority." The Court next found that "the practical effect" of the state initiative was to "remov[e] the authority to address a racial problem—and only a racial problem—from the existing decisionmaking body, in such a way as to burden minority interests" because advocates of busing "now must seek relief from the state legislature, or from the statewide electorate." The Court therefore found that the initiative had "explicitly us[ed] the racial nature of a decision to determine the decisionmaking process."

Seattle is best understood as a case in which the state action in question (the bar on busing enacted by the State's voters) had the serious risk, if not purpose, of causing specific injuries on account of race, just as had been the case in *Mulkey* and *Hunter*. Although there had been no judicial finding of *de jure* segregation with respect to Seattle's school district, it appears as though school segregation in the district in the 1940's and 1950's may have been the partial result of school board policies that "permitted white students to transfer out of black schools while restricting the transfer of black students into white schools." *Parents Involved in Community Schools v. Seattle School Dist. No. 1* (Breyer, J., dissenting). . . .

As this Court held in *Parents Involved,* the school board's purported remedial action would not be permissible today absent a showing of *de jure* segregation. That holding prompted Justice Breyer to observe in dissent, as noted above, that one permissible reading of the record was that the school board had maintained policies to perpetuate racial segregation in the schools. In all events we must understand *Seattle* as *Seattle* understood itself, as a case in which neither the State nor the United States "challenge[d] the propriety of race-conscious student assignments for the purpose of achieving integration, even absent a finding of prior *de jure* segregation." In other words the legitimacy and constitutionality of the remedy in question (busing for desegregation) was assumed, and *Seattle* must be understood on that basis. *Seattle* involved a state initiative that "was carefully tailored to interfere only with desegregative busing." The *Seattle* Court, accepting the validity of the school board's busing remedy as a predicate to its analysis of the constitutional question, found that the State's disapproval of the school

V. Equality and the Constitution

board's busing remedy was an aggravation of the very racial injury in which the State itself was complicit.

The broad language used in *Seattle*, however, went well beyond the analysis needed to resolve the case. [*Seattle*] stated that where a government policy "inures primarily to the benefit of the minority" and "minorities . . . consider" the policy to be " 'in their interest,' " then any state action that "place[s] effective decisionmaking authority over" that policy "at a different level of government" must be reviewed under strict scrutiny. In essence, according to the broad reading of *Seattle*, any state action with a "racial focus" that makes it "more difficult for certain racial minorities than for other groups" to "achieve legislation that is in their interest" is subject to strict scrutiny. It is this reading of *Seattle* that the Court of Appeals found to be controlling here. And that reading must be rejected.

[To] the extent *Seattle* is read to require the Court to determine and declare which political policies serve the "interest" of a group defined in racial terms, that rationale was unnecessary to the decision in *Seattle*; it has no support in precedent; and it raises serious constitutional concerns. That expansive language does not provide a proper guide for decisions and should not be deemed authoritative or controlling. . . .

[It] cannot be entertained as a serious proposition that all individuals of the same race think alike. Yet that proposition would be a necessary beginning point were the *Seattle* formulation to control, as the Court of Appeals held it did in this case. And if it were deemed necessary to probe how some races define their own interest in political matters, still another beginning point would be to define individuals according to race. But in a society in which those lines are becoming more blurred, the attempt to define race-based categories also raises serious questions of its own. Government action that classifies individuals on the basis of race is inherently suspect and carries the danger of perpetuating the very racial divisions the polity seeks to transcend. Were courts to embark upon this venture not only would it be undertaken with no clear legal standards or accepted sources to guide judicial decision but also it would result in, or at least impose a high risk of, inquiries and categories dependent upon demeaning stereotypes, classifications of questionable constitutionality on their own terms.

Even assuming these initial steps could be taken in a manner consistent with a sound analytic and judicial framework, the court would next be required to determine the policy realms in which certain groups—groups defined by race—have a political interest. That undertaking, again without guidance from any accepted legal standards, would risk, in turn, the creation of incentives for those who support or oppose certain policies to cast the debate in terms of racial advantage or disadvantage. Thus could racial antagonisms and conflict tend to arise in the context of judicial decisions as courts undertook to announce what particular issues of public policy should be classified as advantageous to some group defined by race. . . .

[In] a nation in which governmental policies are wide ranging, those who seek to limit voter participation might be tempted, were this Court to adopt the *Seattle* formulation, to urge that a group they choose to define by race or racial stereotypes are advantaged or disadvantaged by any number of laws or decisions. Tax policy, housing subsidies, wage regulations, and even the naming of public schools, highways, and monuments are just a few examples of what could become a list of subjects that some organizations could insist should be beyond the power of voters to decide, or beyond the power of a legislature to decide when enacting limits on the power of local authorities or other governmental entities to address certain subjects. Racial division would be validated, not discouraged, were the *Seattle* formulation, and the reasoning of the Court of Appeals in this case, to remain in force.

[The] holding in the instant case is simply that the courts may not disempower the voters from choosing which path to follow. In the realm of policy discussions the regular give-and-take of debate ought to be a context in which rancor or discord based on race are avoided, not invited. And if these factors are to be interjected, surely it ought not to be at the invitation or insistence of the courts.

One response to these concerns may be that objections to the larger consequences of the *Seattle* formulation need not be confronted in this case, for here race was an undoubted subject of the ballot issue. But a number of problems raised by *Seattle,* such as racial definitions, still apply. And this principal flaw in the ruling of the Court of Appeals does remain: Here there was no infliction of a specific injury of the kind at issue in *Mulkey* and *Hunter* and in the history of the Seattle schools. Here there is no precedent for extending these cases to restrict the right of Michigan voters to determine that race-based preferences granted by Michigan governmental entities should be ended. . . .

By approving Proposal 2 and thereby adding § 26 to their State Constitution, the Michigan voters exercised their privilege to enact laws as a basic exercise of their democratic power. [Michigan] voters used the initiative system to bypass public officials who were deemed not responsive to the concerns of a majority of the voters with respect to a policy of granting race-based preferences that raises difficult and delicate issues.

The freedom secured by the Constitution consists, in one of its essential dimensions, of the right of the individual not to be injured by the unlawful exercise of governmental power. [Yet] freedom does not stop with individual rights. Our constitutional system embraces, too, the right of citizens to debate so they can learn and decide and then, through the political process, act in concert to try to shape the course of their own times and the course of a nation that must strive always to make freedom ever greater and more secure. Here Michigan voters acted in concert and statewide to seek consensus and adopt a policy on a difficult subject against a historical background of race in America that has been a source of tragedy and persisting injustice. That history demands that we continue

V. Equality and the Constitution Page 624

to learn, to listen, and to remain open to new approaches if we are to aspire always to a constitutional order in which all persons are treated with fairness and equal dignity. Were the Court to rule that the question addressed by Michigan voters is too sensitive or complex to be within the grasp of the electorate; or that the policies at issue remain too delicate to be resolved save by university officials or faculties, acting at some remove from immediate public scrutiny and control; or that these matters are so arcane that the electorate's power must be limited because the people cannot prudently exercise that power even after a full debate, that holding would be an unprecedented restriction on the exercise of a fundamental right held not just by one person but by all in common. It is the right to speak and debate and learn and then, as a matter of political will, to act through a lawful electoral process....

It is demeaning to the democratic process to presume that the voters are not capable of deciding an issue of this sensitivity on decent and rational grounds. The process of public discourse and political debate should not be foreclosed even if there is a risk that during a public campaign there will be those, on both sides, who seek to use racial division and discord to their own political advantage. An informed public can, and must, rise above this. The idea of democracy is that it can, and must, mature. Freedom embraces the right, indeed the duty, to engage in a rational, civic discourse in order to determine how best to form a consensus to shape the destiny of the Nation and its people. These First Amendment dynamics would be disserved if this Court were to say that the question here at issue is beyond the capacity of the voters to debate and then to determine.

These precepts are not inconsistent with the well-established principle that when hurt or injury is inflicted on racial minorities by the encouragement or command of laws or other state action, the Constitution requires redress by the courts. As already noted, those were the circumstances that the Court found present in *Mulkey, Hunter*, and *Seattle*. But those circumstances are not present here....

What is at stake here is not whether injury will be inflicted but whether government can be instructed not to follow a course that entails, first, the definition of racial categories and, second, the grant of favored status to persons in some racial categories and not others. The electorate's instruction to governmental entities not to embark upon the course of race-defined and race-based preferences was adopted, we must assume, because the voters deemed a preference system to be unwise, on account of what voters may deem its latent potential to become itself a source of the very resentments and hostilities based on race that this Nation seeks to put behind it. Whether those adverse results would follow is, and should be, the subject of debate. Voters might likewise consider, after debate and reflection, that programs designed to increase diversity — consistent with the Constitution — are a necessary part of progress to transcend the stigma of past racism.

This case is not about how the debate about racial preferences should be resolved. It is about who may resolve it. There is no authority in the Constitution of the United States or in this Court's precedents for the Judiciary to set aside Michigan laws that commit this policy determination to the voters. Deliberative debate on sensitive issues such as racial preferences all too often may shade into rancor. But that does not justify removing certain court-determined issues from the voters' reach. Democracy does not presume that some subjects are either too divisive or too profound for public debate. . . .

JUSTICE KAGAN took no part in the consideration or decision of this case.

CHIEF JUSTICE ROBERTS, concurring.

The dissent devotes 11 pages to expounding its own policy preferences in favor of taking race into account in college admissions, while nonetheless concluding that it "do[es] not mean to suggest that the virtues of adopting race-sensitive admissions policies should inform the legal question before the Court." The dissent concedes that the governing boards of the State's various universities could have implemented a policy making it illegal to "discriminate against, or grant preferential treatment to," any individual on the basis of race. On the dissent's view, if the governing boards conclude that drawing racial distinctions in university admissions is undesirable or counterproductive, they are permissibly exercising their policymaking authority. But others who might reach the same conclusion are failing to take race seriously.

The dissent states that "[t]he way to stop discrimination on the basis of race is to speak openly and candidly on the subject of race." And it urges that "[r]ace matters because of the slights, the snickers, the silent judgments that reinforce that most crippling of thoughts: 'I do not belong here.'" But it is not "out of touch with reality" to conclude that racial preferences may themselves have the debilitating effect of reinforcing precisely that doubt, and—if so—that the preferences do more harm than good. To disagree with the dissent's views on the costs and benefits of racial preferences is not to "wish away, rather than confront" racial inequality. People can disagree in good faith on this issue, but it similarly does more harm than good to question the openness and candor of those on either side of the debate.

JUSTICE SCALIA, with whom JUSTICE THOMAS joins, concurring in the judgment.

It has come to this. Called upon to explore the jurisprudential twilight zone between two errant lines of precedent, we confront a frighteningly bizarre question: Does the Equal Protection Clause of the Fourteenth Amendment *forbid* what its text plainly *requires*? Needless to say (except that this case obliges us to say it), the question answers itself. "The Constitution proscribes government discrimination on the basis of race, and state-provided education is no exception." [*Grutter* (Scalia, J., concurring in part and dissenting in part)]. It is precisely this understanding—the correct understanding—of the federal Equal Protection Clause

V. Equality and the Constitution

that the people of the State of Michigan have adopted for their own fundamental law. By adopting it, they did not simultaneously *offend* it.

Even taking this Court's sorry line of race-based-admissions cases as a given, I find the question presented only slightly less strange: Does the Equal Protection Clause forbid a State from banning a practice that the Clause barely—and only provisionally—permits? Reacting to those race-based-admissions decisions, some States—whether deterred by the prospect of costly litigation; aware that *Grutter*'s bell may soon toll; or simply opposed in principle to the notion of "benign" racial discrimination—have gotten out of the racial-preferences business altogether. And with our express encouragement: "Universities in California, Florida, and Washington State, where racial preferences in admissions are prohibited by state law, are currently engaging in experimenting with a wide variety of alternative approaches. Universities in other States can *and should* draw on the most promising aspects of these race-neutral alternatives as they develop." (emphasis added). Respondents seem to think this admonition was merely in jest. The experiment, they maintain, is not only over; it never rightly began. Neither the people of the States nor their legislatures ever had the option of directing subordinate public-university officials to cease considering the race of applicants, since that would deny members of those minority groups the option of enacting a policy designed to further their interest, thus denying them the equal protection of the laws. Never mind that it is hotly disputed whether the practice of race-based admissions is *ever* in a racial minority's interest. And never mind that, were a public university to stake its defense of a race-based-admissions policy on the ground that it was *designed* to benefit primarily minorities (as opposed to all students, regardless of color, by enhancing diversity), *we would hold the policy unconstitutional*.

But the battleground for this case is not the constitutionality of race-based admissions—at least, not quite. Rather, it is the so-called political-process doctrine, derived from this Court's opinions in *Washington v. Seattle School Dist. No. 1,* and *Hunter v. Erickson.* I agree with those parts of the plurality opinion that repudiate this doctrine. But I do not agree with its reinterpretation of *Seattle* and *Hunter*, which makes them stand in part for the cloudy and doctrinally anomalous proposition that whenever state action poses "the serious risk . . . of causing specific injuries on account of race," it denies equal protection. I would instead reaffirm that the "ordinary principles of our law [and] of our democratic heritage" require "plaintiffs alleging equal protection violations" stemming from facially neutral acts to "prove intent and causation and not merely the existence of racial disparity." Freeman v. Pitts, 503 U.S. 467, 506 (Scalia, J., concurring) (citing Washington v. Davis, 426 U.S. 229 (1976)). I would further hold that a law directing state actors to provide equal protection is (to say the least) facially neutral, and cannot violate the Constitution. Section 26 of the Michigan Constitution (formerly Proposal 2) rightly stands. . . .

[*Hunter, Seattle,* and, I think, the plurality endorse a version of the proposition that a facially neutral law may deny equal protection solely because it has a disparate racial impact. Few equal-protection theories have been so squarely and soundly rejected. . . .

Notwithstanding our dozens of cases confirming the exceptionless nature of the *Washington v. Davis* rule, the plurality opinion leaves ajar an effects-test escape hatch modeled after *Hunter* and *Seattle*, suggesting that state action denies equal protection when it "ha[s] the *serious risk,* if not purpose, of causing specific injuries on account of race," or is either "designed to be used, or . . . *likely to be used,* to encourage infliction of injury by reason of race." (emphasis added). Since these formulations enable a determination of an equal-protection violation where there is no discriminatory intent, they are inconsistent with the long *Washington v. Davis* line of cases. . . .

Thus, the question in this case, as in every case in which neutral state action is said to deny equal protection on account of race, is whether the action reflects a racially discriminatory purpose. *Seattle* stresses that "singling out the political processes affecting racial issues for uniquely disadvantageous treatment inevitably raises dangers of impermissible motivation." True enough, but that motivation must be proved. And respondents do not have a prayer of proving it here. The District Court noted that, under "conventional equal protection" doctrine, the suit was "doom[ed]." Though the Court of Appeals did not opine on this question, I would not leave it for them on remand. In my view, any law expressly requiring state actors to afford all persons equal protection of the laws (such as Initiative 350 in *Seattle*, though not the charter amendment in *Hunter*) does not—cannot—deny "to any person . . . equal protection of the laws," U.S. Const., Amdt. 14, § 1, regardless of whatever evidence of seemingly foul purposes plaintiffs may cook up in the trial court.

* * *

As Justice Harlan observed over a century ago, "[o]ur Constitution is colorblind, and neither knows nor tolerates classes among citizens." (dissenting opinion). The people of Michigan wish the same for their governing charter. It would be shameful for us to stand in their way.[11]

JUSTICE BREYER, concurring in the judgment. . . .

I agree with the plurality that the amendment is consistent with the Federal Equal Protection Clause. But I believe this for different reasons.

---

11. And doubly shameful to equate "the majority" behind § 26 with "the majority" responsible for Jim Crow. (Sotomayor, J., dissenting).

[We] do not address the amendment insofar as it forbids the use of race-conscious admissions programs designed to remedy past exclusionary racial discrimination or the direct effects of that discrimination. Application of the amendment in that context would present different questions which may demand different answers....

I continue to believe that the Constitution permits, though it does not require, the use of the kind of race-conscious programs that are now barred by the Michigan Constitution....

The Constitution allows local, state, and national communities to adopt narrowly tailored race-conscious programs designed to bring about greater inclusion and diversity. But the Constitution foresees the ballot box, not the courts, as the normal instrument for resolving differences and debates about the merits of these programs.

[Cases] such as *Hunter v. Erickson* and *Washington v. Seattle School Dist. No. 1* reflect an important principle, namely, that an individual's ability to participate meaningfully in the political process should be independent of his race. Although racial minorities, like other political minorities, will not always succeed at the polls, they must have the same opportunity as others to secure through the ballot box policies that reflect their preferences. In my view, however, neither *Hunter* nor *Seattle* applies here. And the parties do not here suggest that the amendment violates the Equal Protection Clause if not under the *Hunter-Seattle* doctrine.

[*Hunter* and *Seattle*] involved a restructuring of the political process that changed the political level at which policies were enacted. In *Hunter*, decisionmaking was moved from the elected city council to the local electorate at large. And in *Seattle*, decisionmaking by an elected school board was replaced with decisionmaking by the state legislature and electorate at large.

This case, in contrast, does not involve a reordering of the *political* process; it does not in fact involve the movement of decisionmaking from one political level to another. Rather, here, Michigan law delegated broad policymaking authority to elected university boards, but those boards delegated admissions-related decisionmaking authority to unelected university faculty members and administrators. Although the boards unquestionably retained the *power* to set policy regarding race-conscious admissions, in *fact* faculty members and administrators set the race-conscious admissions policies in question. [Thus], unelected faculty members and administrators, not voters or their elected representatives, adopted the race-conscious admissions programs affected by Michigan's constitutional amendment. The amendment took decisionmaking authority away from these unelected actors and placed it in the hands of the voters.

[The] doctrine set forth in *Hunter* and *Seattle* does not easily fit this case. In those cases minorities had participated in the political process and they had won. The majority's subsequent reordering of the political process repealed the minority's successes and made it more difficult for the minority to succeed in

57

the future. [But] one cannot as easily characterize the movement of the decisionmaking mechanism at issue here—from an administrative process to an electoral process—as diminishing the minority's ability to participate meaningfully in the *political* process. There is no prior electoral process in which the minority participated.

For another thing, to extend the holding of *Hunter* and *Seattle* to reach situations in which decisionmaking authority is moved from an administrative body to a political one would pose significant difficulties. The administrative process encompasses vast numbers of decisionmakers answering numerous policy questions in hosts of different fields. Administrative bodies modify programs in detail, and decisionmaking authority within the administrative process frequently moves around—due to amendments to statutes, new administrative rules, and evolving agency practice. It is thus particularly difficult in this context for judges to determine when a change in the locus of decisionmaking authority places a comparative structural burden on a racial minority. And to apply *Hunter* and *Seattle* to the administrative process would, by tending to hinder change, risk discouraging experimentation, interfering with efforts to see when and how race-conscious policies work.

Finally, the principle that underlies *Hunter* and *Seattle* runs up against a competing principle, discussed above. This competing principle favors decisionmaking [through] the democratic process. Just as this principle strongly supports the right of the people, or their elected representatives, to adopt race-conscious policies for reasons of inclusion, so must it give them the right to vote not to do so....

JUSTICE SOTOMAYOR, with whom JUSTICE GINSBURG joins, dissenting.

We are fortunate to live in a democratic society. But without checks, democratically approved legislation can oppress minority groups. For that reason, our Constitution places limits on what a majority of the people may do. This case implicates one such limit: the guarantee of equal protection of the laws. Although that guarantee is traditionally understood to prohibit intentional discrimination under existing laws, equal protection does not end there. Another fundamental strand of our equal protection jurisprudence focuses on process, securing to all citizens the right to participate meaningfully and equally in self-government. That right is the bedrock of our democracy, for it preserves all other rights.

Yet to know the history of our Nation is to understand its long and lamentable record of stymieing the right of racial minorities to participate in the political process. At first, the majority acted with an open, invidious purpose. Notwithstanding the command of the Fifteenth Amendment, certain States shut racial minorities out of the political process altogether by withholding the right to vote. This Court intervened to preserve that right. The majority tried again, replacing outright bans on voting with literacy tests, good character requirements, poll taxes, and gerrymandering. The Court was not fooled; it invalidated those measures, too. The majority persisted. This time, although it allowed the minority access to the political process, the majority changed the ground rules of the process so as to make it more difficult for the minority, and the minority alone, to obtain policies designed to foster racial integration. Although these political restructurings may not have been discriminatory in purpose, the Court reaffirmed the right of minority members of our society to participate meaningfully and equally in the political process.

This case involves this last chapter of discrimination: A majority of the Michigan electorate changed the basic rules of the political process in that State in a manner that uniquely disadvantaged racial minorities.[1] Prior to the enactment of the constitutional initiative at issue here, all of the admissions policies of Michigan's public colleges and universities—including race-sensitive admissions policies—were in the hands of each institution's governing board. The members of those boards are nominated by political parties and elected by the citizenry in statewide elections. After over a century of being shut out of Michigan's institutions of higher education, racial minorities in Michigan had succeeded in persuading the elected board representatives to adopt admissions policies that took into account the benefits of racial diversity. And this Court twice blessed such efforts—first in *Regents of Univ. of Cal. v. Bakke,* and again in *Grutter v. Bollinger,* a case that itself concerned a Michigan admissions policy.

In the wake of *Grutter,* some voters in Michigan set out to eliminate the use of race-sensitive admissions policies. Those voters were of course free to pursue this end in any number of ways. For example, they could have persuaded existing board members to change their minds through individual or grassroots lobbying efforts, or through general public awareness campaigns. Or they could have mobilized efforts to vote uncooperative board members out of office, replacing them with members who would share their desire to abolish race-sensitive admissions policies. When this Court holds that the Constitution permits a particular policy, nothing prevents a majority of a State's voters from choosing not to adopt that policy. Our system of government encourages—and indeed, depends on—that type of democratic action.

But instead, the majority of Michigan voters changed the rules in the middle of the game, reconfiguring the existing political process in Michigan in a manner that burdened racial minorities. They did so in the 2006 election by amending the Michigan [Constitution].

---

1. I of course do not mean to suggest that Michigan's voters acted with anything like the invidious intent, of those who historically stymied the rights of racial minorities. Contra, n. 11 (Scalia, J., concurring in judgment). But like earlier chapters of political restructuring, the Michigan amendment at issue in this case changed the rules of the political process to the disadvantage of minority members of our society.

As a result of § 26, there are now two very different processes through which a Michigan citizen is permitted to influence the admissions policies of the State's universities: one for persons interested in race-sensitive admissions policies and one for everyone else. A citizen who is a University of Michigan alumnus, for instance, can advocate for an admissions policy that considers an applicant's legacy status by meeting individually with members of the Board of Regents to convince them of her views, by joining with other legacy parents to lobby the Board, or by voting for and supporting Board candidates who share her position. The same options are available to a citizen who wants the Board to adopt admissions policies that consider athleticism, geography, area of study, and so on. The one and only policy a Michigan citizen may not seek through this long-established process is a race-sensitive admissions policy that considers race in an individualized manner when it is clear that race-neutral alternatives are not adequate to achieve diversity. For that policy alone, the citizens of Michigan must undertake the daunting task of amending the State Constitution.

Our precedents do not permit political restructurings that create one process for racial minorities and a separate, less burdensome process for everyone else....

Today, disregarding *stare decisis,* a majority of the Court effectively discards those precedents. The plurality does so, it tells us, because the freedom actually secured by the Constitution is the freedom of self-government—because the majority of Michigan citizens "exercised their privilege to enact laws as a basic exercise of their democratic power." It would be "demeaning to the democratic process," the plurality concludes, to disturb that decision in any way. This logic embraces majority rule without an important constitutional limit.

The plurality's decision fundamentally misunderstands the nature of the injustice worked by § 26. This case is not, as the plurality imagines, about "who may resolve" the debate over the use of race in higher education admissions. I agree wholeheartedly that nothing vests the resolution of that debate exclusively in the courts or requires that we remove it from the reach of the electorate. Rather, this case is about *how* the debate over the use of race-sensitive admissions policies may be resolved—that is, it must be resolved in constitutionally permissible ways. While our Constitution does not guarantee minority groups victory in the political process, it does guarantee them meaningful and equal access to that process. It guarantees that the majority may not win by stacking the political process against minority groups permanently, forcing the minority alone to surmount unique obstacles in pursuit of its goals—here, educational diversity that cannot reasonably be accomplished through race-neutral measures. Today, by permitting a majority of the voters in Michigan to do what our Constitution forbids, the Court ends the debate over race-sensitive admissions policies in Michigan in a manner that contravenes constitutional protections long recognized in our precedents.

Like the plurality, I have faith that our citizenry will continue to learn from this Nation's regrettable history; that it will strive to move beyond those injustices towards a future of equality. And I, too, believe in the importance of public discourse on matters of public policy. But I part ways with the plurality when it suggests that judicial intervention in this case "impede[s]" rather than "advance[s]" the democratic process and the ultimate hope of equality. I firmly believe that our role as judges includes policing the process of self-government and stepping in when necessary to secure the constitutional guarantee of equal protection. Because I would do so here, I respectfully dissent. . . .

Section 26 has a "racial focus." *Seattle.* That is clear from its text, which prohibits Michigan's public colleges and universities from "grant[ing] preferential treatment to any individual or group on the basis of race." Like desegregation of public schools, race-sensitive admissions policies "inur[e] primarily to the benefit of the minority," [*Seattle,*] as they are designed to increase minorities' access to institutions of higher education.

Petitioner argues that race-sensitive admissions policies cannot "inur[e] primarily to the benefit of the minority," as the Court has upheld such policies only insofar as they further "the educational benefits that flow from a diverse student body," [*Grutter.*] But there is no conflict between this Court's pronouncement in *Grutter* and the common-sense reality that race-sensitive admissions policies benefit minorities. Rather, race-sensitive admissions policies further a compelling state interest in achieving a diverse student body precisely because they increase minority enrollment, which necessarily benefits minority groups. In other words, constitutionally permissible race-sensitive admissions policies can both serve the compelling interest of obtaining the educational benefits that flow from a diverse student body, and inure to the benefit of racial minorities. . . .

Section 26 restructures the political process in Michigan in a manner that places unique burdens on racial minorities. It establishes a distinct and more burdensome political process for the enactment of admissions plans that consider racial diversity. . . .

The plurality sees it differently. [According] to the plurality, the *Hunter* and *Seattle* Courts were not concerned with efforts to reconfigure the political process to the detriment of racial minorities; rather, those cases invalidated governmental actions merely because they reflected an invidious purpose to discriminate. This is not a tenable reading of those cases.

The plurality identifies "invidious discrimination" as the "necessary result" of the restructuring in *Hunter.* It is impossible to assess whether the housing amendment in *Hunter* was motivated by discriminatory purpose, for the opinion does not discuss the question of intent. What is obvious, however, is that the possibility of invidious discrimination played no role in the Court's reasoning. We ordinarily understand our precedents to mean what they actually say, not what we later think they could or should have said. The *Hunter* Court was clear about why it invalidated the Akron charter amendment: It was impermissible as a restructuring of the political process, not as an action motivated by discriminatory intent.

Similarly, the plurality disregards what *Seattle* actually says and instead opines that "the political restriction in question was designed to be used, or was likely to be used, to encourage infliction of injury by reason of race." Here, the plurality derives its conclusion not from *Seattle* itself, but from evidence unearthed more than a quarter-century later in *Parents Involved in Community Schools v. Seattle School Dist. No. 1*. . . .

Not once did the [*Seattle*] Court suggest the presence of *de jure* segregation in Seattle. Quite the opposite: The opinion explicitly suggested the desegregation plan was adopted to remedy *de facto* rather than *de jure* segregation. The Court, moreover, assumed that no "constitutional violation" through *de jure* segregation had occurred. And it unmistakably rested its decision on *Hunter*, holding Seattle's initiative invalid because it "use[d] the racial nature of an issue to define the governmental decisionmaking structure, and thus impose[d] substantial and unique burdens on racial minorities." . . .

[Justice] Scalia disagrees with "the proposition that a facially neutral law may deny equal protection solely because it has a disparate racial impact." (opinion concurring in judgment). He would acknowledge, however, that an act that draws racial distinctions or makes racial classifications triggers strict scrutiny regardless of whether discriminatory intent is shown. That should settle the matter: Section 26 draws a racial distinction. As the *Seattle* Court explained, "when the political process or the decisionmaking mechanism used to *address* racially conscious legislation—and only such legislation—is singled out for peculiar and disadvantageous treatment, the governmental action plainly rests on 'distinctions based on race.'" . . .

My colleagues are of the view that we should leave race out of the picture entirely and let the voters sort it out. We have seen this reasoning before. See *Parents Involved* ("The way to stop discrimination on the basis of race is to stop discriminating on the basis of race"). It is a sentiment out of touch with reality, one not required by our Constitution, and one that has properly been rejected as "not sufficient" to resolve cases of this nature. Id. (Kennedy, J., concurring in part and concurring in judgment). While "[t]he enduring hope is that race should not matter[,] the reality is that too often it does." Id. "[R]acial discrimination . . . [is] not ancient history." Bartlett v. Strickland, 556 U.S. 1, 25 (2009) (plurality opinion).

Race matters. Race matters in part because of the long history of racial minorities' being denied access to the political process. And although we have made great strides, "voting discrimination still exists; no one doubts that." [Shelby Cnty. v. Holder, 133 S. Ct. 2612, 2619 (2012)].

Race also matters because of persistent racial inequality in society—inequality that cannot be ignored and that has produced stark socioeconomic disparities. . . .

V. Equality and the Constitution   Page 624

And race matters for reasons that really are only skin deep, that cannot be discussed any other way, and that cannot be wished away. Race matters to a young man's view of society when he spends his teenage years watching others tense up as he passes, no matter the neighborhood where he grew up. Race matters to a young woman's sense of self when she states her hometown, and then is pressed, "No, where are you *really* from?", regardless of how many generations her family has been in the country. Race matters to a young person addressed by a stranger in a foreign language, which he does not understand because only English was spoken at home. Race matters because of the slights, the snickers, the silent judgments that reinforce that most crippling of thoughts: "I do not belong here."

In my colleagues' view, examining the racial impact of legislation only perpetuates racial discrimination. This refusal to accept the stark reality that race matters is regrettable. The way to stop discrimination on the basis of race is to speak openly and candidly on the subject of race, and to apply the Constitution with eyes open to the unfortunate effects of centuries of racial discrimination. As members of the judiciary tasked with intervening to carry out the guarantee of equal protection, we ought not sit back and wish away, rather than confront, the racial inequality that exists in our society. It is this view that works harm, by perpetuating the facile notion that what makes race matter is acknowledging the simple truth that race *does* matter. . . .

V

Although the only constitutional rights at stake in this case are process-based rights, the substantive policy at issue is undeniably of some relevance to my colleagues. I will therefore speak in response. . . .

[Justice Sotomayor outlines the history of segregation in Michigan's colleges and universities, the growing diversity of the student population during the period when the state used "race-sensitive" admissions policies, and the decline in diversity in Michigan and elsewhere after abandonment of "race-sensitive" policies.]

These statistics may not influence the views of some of my colleagues, as they question the wisdom of adopting race-sensitive admissions policies and would prefer if our Nation's colleges and universities were to discard those policies altogether. See (Roberts, C.J., concurring) (suggesting that race-sensitive admissions policies might "do more harm than good"); (Scalia, J., concurring in judgment); *Grutter* (Thomas, J., concurring in part and dissenting in part); id. (Scalia, J., concurring in part and dissenting in part). That view is at odds with our recognition in *Grutter,* and more recently in *Fisher v. University of Texas at Austin,* that race-sensitive admissions policies are necessary to achieve a diverse student body when race-neutral alternatives have failed. More fundamentally, it ignores the importance of diversity in institutions of higher education and reveals how little my colleagues understand about the reality of race in America. . . .

To be clear, I do not mean to suggest that the virtues of adopting race-sensitive admissions policies should inform the legal question before the Court today regarding the constitutionality of § 26. But I cannot ignore the unfortunate outcome of today's decision: Short of amending the State Constitution, a Herculean task, racial minorities in Michigan are deprived of even an opportunity to convince Michigan's public colleges and universities to consider race in their admissions plans when other attempts to achieve racial diversity have proved unworkable, and those institutions are unnecessarily hobbled in their pursuit of a diverse student body. . . .

Today's decision eviscerates an important strand of our equal protection jurisprudence. For members of historically marginalized groups, which rely on the federal courts to protect their constitutional rights, the decision can hardly bolster hope for a vision of democracy that preserves for all the right to participate meaningfully and equally in self-government.

I respectfully dissent.

Page 628. Before section 4 of the Note, add the following:

3a. *Affirmative action, democracy, and the standard of review.* Note the *Schuette* Court's view that "[it] is demeaning to the democratic process to presume that the voters are not capable of deciding an issue of this sensitivity on decent and rational grounds" and that "[freedom] embraces the right, indeed the duty, to engage in a rational, civic discourse in order to determine how best to form a consensus to shape the destiny of the Nation and its people." Is this position consistent with the Court's insistence on strictly scrutinizing decisions by the political branches to adopt affirmative action programs? Is the Court's insistence on strict scrutiny for these programs, even when their purpose is benign, consistent with its use of rational basis review when a facially neutral statute harms racial minorities for benign purposes?

Siegel, Foreword: Equality Divided, 127 Harv. L. Rev. 1, 50 (2013), argues that "[equal] protection doctrine governing affirmative action worries about the racial meaning and impact of state action even when the government has compelling purposes; but the [illegitimate purpose framework for *Feeney* (discussed at page 544 of the main volume)] makes the impact of state action on adversely affected communities immaterial unless the plaintiffs can show that the government acted, at least in part, for the purpose of inflicting the adverse impact on them." Siegel concludes that the Court has thereby turned its traditional *Carolene Products* approach inside out to create "a form of judicial review that cares more about protecting members of majority groups from actions of representative government that promote minority opportunities than it cares about protecting

V. Equality and the Constitution   Page 689

'discrete and insular minorities' from actions of representative government that reflect 'prejudice.'" Does this approach place too little weight on the fact that affirmative action programs make facial distinctions whereas programs like the one upheld in *Feeney* are facially neutral? If so, why is this difference so significant?

E. *The Problem of Sexual Orientation*

Page 689. At the end of the block quote, add the following:

The Supreme Court affirmed *Windsor* in United States v. Windsor, 133 S. Ct. 2675 (2013). The opinions in the case are excerpted in Chapter VI F 3 of this Supplement. Justice Kennedy, writing for the Court's majority, stated that "[t]he liberty protected by the Fifth Amendment's Due Process Clause contains within it the prohibition against denying to any person the equal protection of the laws. While the Fifth Amendment itself withdraws from Government the power to degrade or demean in the way this law does, the equal protection guarantee of the Fourteenth Amendment makes that Fifth Amendment right all the more specific and all the better understood and preserved." The majority opinion does not discuss the appropriate standard of review. Consider the following excerpt from Justice Alito's dissenting opinion:

> Our equal protection framework, upon which Windsor and the United States rely, is a judicial construct that provides a useful mechanism for analyzing a certain universe of equal protection cases. But that framework is ill suited for use in evaluating the constitutionality of laws based on the traditional understanding of marriage, which fundamentally turn on what marriage is. . . .
>
> In asking the Court to determine that § 3 of DOMA is subject to and violates heightened scrutiny, Windsor and the United States thus ask us to rule that the presence of two members of the opposite sex is as rationally related to marriage as white skin is to voting or a Y-chromosome is to the ability to administer an estate. That is a striking request and one that unelected judges should pause before granting. Acceptance of the argument would cast all those who cling to traditional beliefs about the nature of marriage in the role of bigots or superstitious fools.
>
> By asking the Court to strike down DOMA as not satisfying some form of heightened scrutiny, Windsor and the United States are really seeking to have the Court resolve a debate between two competing views of marriage.

The first and older view, which I will call the "traditional" or "conjugal" view, sees marriage as an intrinsically opposite-sex institution. BLAG notes that virtually every culture, including many not influenced by the Abrahamic religions, has limited marriage to people of the opposite sex. And BLAG attempts to explain this phenomenon by arguing that the institution of marriage was created for the purpose of channeling heterosexual intercourse into a structure that supports child rearing. Others explain the basis for the institution in more philosophical terms. They argue that marriage is essentially the solemnizing of a comprehensive, exclusive, permanent union that is intrinsically ordered to producing new life, even if it does not always do so. While modern cultural changes have weakened the link between marriage and procreation in the popular mind, there is no doubt that, throughout human history and across many cultures, marriage has been viewed as an exclusively opposite-sex institution and as one inextricably linked to procreation and biological kinship.

The other, newer view is what I will call the "consent-based" vision of marriage, a vision that primarily defines marriage as the solemnization of mutual commitment—marked by strong emotional attachment and sexual attraction—between two persons. At least as it applies to heterosexual couples, this view of marriage now plays a very prominent role in the popular understanding of the institution. Indeed, our popular culture is infused with this understanding of marriage. Proponents of same-sex marriage argue that because gender differentiation is not relevant to this vision, the exclusion of same-sex couples from the institution of marriage is rank discrimination.

The Constitution does not codify either of these views of marriage (although I suspect it would have been hard at the time of the adoption of the Constitution or the Fifth Amendment to find Americans who did not take the traditional view for granted). The silence of the Constitution on this question should be enough to end the matter as far as the judiciary is concerned. Yet, Windsor and the United States implicitly ask us to endorse the consent-based view of marriage and to reject the traditional view, thereby arrogating to ourselves the power to decide a question that philosophers, historians, social scientists, and theologians are better qualified to explore. Because our constitutional order assigns the resolution of questions of this nature to the people, I would not presume to enshrine either vision of marriage in our constitutional jurisprudence. . . .

F. Other Candidates for Heightened Scrutiny

Page 719. At the end of the Note, add the following:

Consider Pollvogt, Beyond Suspect Classifications, 16 U. Pa. J. Const. L. 739, 798 (2014): "[Suspect] classification analysis asks the wrong question and scrutinizes the wrong actor. [The] approach relies on a questionable assumption that the Court can properly identify social and political marginalization, and [contemporary] prejudices." Instead of asking questions about group marginalization, prejudice, and political power, Pollvogt suggests the following test for all classifications: "Where a law or other government action relies on a facial classification of persons the burden is on the government to prove an affirmative connection between the trait that defines the targeted group and the governmental and individual interests being regulated." Note that this test does not specify the necessary degree of fit between the classification and the trait or how heavy the government's burden should be. Does answering those questions lead back to suspect classification analysis?

VI
IMPLIED FUNDAMENTAL RIGHTS

F. Modern Substantive Due Process: Privacy, Personhood, and Family

2. Abortion.

Page 900. At the end of the last full paragraph on the page, add the following:

As respondents have noted, and the District Courts recognized, some recitations in the Act are factually incorrect. Whether or not accurate at the time, some of the important findings have been superseded. Two examples suffice. Congress determined no medical schools provide instruction on the prohibited procedure. The testimony in the District Courts, however, demonstrated intact D & E is taught at medical schools. Congress also found there existed a medical consensus that the prohibited procedure is never medically necessary. The evidence presented in the District Courts contradicts that conclusion. Uncritical deference to Congress's factual findings in these cases is inappropriate.

3. Family and Other Privacy Interests

Page 937. At the end of the Note, add the following:

UNITED STATES v. WINDSOR
133 S. Ct. 2675 (2013)

JUSTICE KENNEDY delivered the opinion of the Court.

I

[Section 3 of the Defense of Marriage Act, 1 U.S.C. § 7 (DOMA) provides:

> In determining the meaning of any Act of Congress, or of any ruling, regulation, or interpretation of the various administrative bureaus and agencies of the United States, the word "marriage" means only a legal union between one man and one woman as husband and wife, and the word "spouse" refers only to a person of the opposite sex who is a husband or a wife.

This provision controls over 1,000 federal laws whose coverage turns on marital status.

Respondent Edith Windsor married Thea Spyer in Canada in 2007. The couple lived in New York, which recognized their marriage, until Spyer died in 2009. Spyer left her estate to Windsor but, because DOMA denied federal recognition to same-sex spouses, Windsor did not qualify for the marital exemption from the federal estate tax. Windsor was therefore compelled to pay $363,053, which she would not have owed if she had been married to a man.]

II

[In this section of the opinion, the Court holds that the case is properly before it. This holding is discussed in Chapter 1 F 2 of this Supplement.]

III

[It] seems fair to conclude that, until recent years, many citizens had not even considered the possibility that two persons of the same sex might aspire to occupy the same status and dignity as that of a man and woman in lawful marriage. For marriage between a man and a woman no doubt had been thought of by most people as essential to the very definition of that term and to its role and function throughout the history of civilization. That belief, for many who long have held it, became even more urgent, more cherished when challenged. For others, however, came the beginnings of a new perspective, a new insight. Accordingly some States concluded that same-sex marriage ought to be given recognition and validity in the law for those same-sex couples who wish to define themselves by their commitment to each other. The limitation of lawful marriage to heterosexual couples, which for centuries had been deemed both necessary and fundamental, came to be seen in New York and certain other States as an unjust exclusion. . . .

Against this background of lawful same-sex marriage in some States, the design, purpose, and effect of DOMA should be considered as the beginning point in deciding whether it is valid under the Constitution. By history and tradition the definition and regulation of marriage [has] been treated as being within

VI. Implied Fundamental Rights   Page 937

the authority and realm of the separate States. Yet it is further established that Congress, in enacting discrete statutes, can make determinations that bear on marital rights and privileges. . . .

Though these discrete examples establish the constitutionality of limited federal laws that regulate the meaning of marriage in order to further federal policy, DOMA has a far greater reach; for it enacts a directive applicable to over 1,000 federal statutes and the whole realm of federal regulations. And its operation is directed to a class of persons that the laws of New York, and of 11 other States, have sought to protect. . . .

In order to assess the validity of that intervention it is necessary to discuss the extent of the state power and authority over marriage as a matter of history and tradition. State laws defining and regulating marriage, of course, must respect the constitutional rights of persons, see, *e.g.,* [*Loving v. Virginia*]; but, subject to those guarantees, "regulation of domestic relations" is "an area that has long been regarded as a virtually exclusive province of the States." . . .

Against this background DOMA rejects the long-established precept that the incidents, benefits, and obligations of marriage are uniform for all married couples within each State, though they may vary, subject to constitutional guarantees, from one State to the next. Despite these considerations, it is unnecessary to decide whether this federal intrusion on state power is a violation of the Constitution because it disrupts the federal balance. The State's power in defining the marital relation is of central relevance in this case quite apart from principles of federalism. Here the State's decision to give this class of persons the right to marry conferred upon them a dignity and status of immense import. When the State used its historic and essential authority to define the marital relation in this way, its role and its power in making the decision enhanced the recognition, dignity, and protection of the class in their own community. DOMA, because of its reach and extent, departs from this history and tradition of reliance on state law to define marriage. "'[D]iscriminations of an unusual character especially suggest careful consideration to determine whether they are obnoxious to the constitutional provision.'" [*Romer v. Evans.*]

The Federal Government uses this state-defined class for the opposite purpose—to impose restrictions and disabilities. That result requires this Court now to address whether the resulting injury and indignity is a deprivation of an essential part of the liberty protected by the Fifth Amendment. What the State of New York treats as alike the federal law deems unlike by a law designed to injure the same class the State seeks to protect. . . .

The States' interest in defining and regulating the marital relation, subject to constitutional guarantees, stems from the understanding that marriage is more than a routine classification for purposes of certain statutory benefits. Private, consensual sexual intimacy between two adult persons of the same sex may not be punished by the State, and it can form "but one element in a personal bond that

71

is more enduring." [*Lawrence v. Texas*.] By its recognition of the validity of same-sex marriages performed in other jurisdictions and then by authorizing same-sex unions and same-sex marriages, New York sought to give further protection and dignity to that bond. For same-sex couples who wished to be married, the State acted to give their lawful conduct a lawful status. This status is a far-reaching legal acknowledgment of the intimate relationship between two people, a relationship deemed by the State worthy of dignity in the community equal with all other marriages. It reflects both the community's considered perspective on the historical roots of the institution of marriage and its evolving understanding of the meaning of equality.

IV

DOMA seeks to injure the very class New York seeks to protect. By doing so it violates basic due process and equal protection principles applicable to the Federal Government. See U.S. Const., Amdt. 5; Bolling v. Sharpe, 347 U.S. 497 (1954). The Constitution's guarantee of equality "must at the very least mean that a bare congressional desire to harm a politically unpopular group cannot" justify disparate treatment of that group. [*Department of Agriculture v. Marino*.] In determining whether a law is motived by an improper animus or purpose, "'[d]iscriminations of an unusual character'" especially require careful consideration. DOMA cannot survive under these principles. The responsibility of the States for the regulation of domestic relations is an important indicator of the substantial societal impact the State's classifications have in the daily lives and customs of its people. DOMA's unusual deviation from the usual tradition of recognizing and accepting state definitions of marriage here operates to deprive same-sex couples of the benefits and responsibilities that come with the federal recognition of their marriages. This is strong evidence of a law having the purpose and effect of disapproval of that class. The avowed purpose and practical effect of the law here in question are to impose a disadvantage, a separate status, and so a stigma upon all who enter into same-sex marriages made lawful by the unquestioned authority of the States.

The history of DOMA's enactment and its own text demonstrate that interference with the equal dignity of same-sex marriages, a dignity conferred by the States in the exercise of their sovereign power, was more than an incidental effect of the federal statute. It was its essence. The House Report announced its conclusion that "it is both appropriate and necessary for Congress to do what it can to defend the institution of traditional heterosexual marriage.... H.R. 3396 is appropriately entitled the 'Defense of Marriage Act.' The effort to redefine 'marriage' to extend to homosexual couples is a truly radical proposal that would fundamentally alter the institution of marriage." The House concluded that DOMA expresses "both moral disapproval of homosexuality, and a moral conviction

VI. Implied Fundamental Rights

that heterosexuality better comports with traditional (especially Judeo-Christian) morality." The stated purpose of the law was to promote an "interest in protecting the traditional moral teachings reflected in heterosexual-only marriage laws." Were there any doubt of this far-reaching purpose, the title of the Act confirms it: The Defense of Marriage. . . .

The Act's demonstrated purpose is to ensure that if any State decides to recognize same-sex marriages, those unions will be treated as second-class marriages for purposes of federal law. This raises a most serious question under the Constitution's Fifth Amendment.

DOMA's operation in practice confirms this purpose. When New York adopted a law to permit same-sex marriage, it sought to eliminate inequality; but DOMA frustrates that objective through a system-wide enactment with no identified connection to any particular area of federal law. DOMA writes inequality into the entire United States Code. The particular case at hand concerns the estate tax, but DOMA is more than a simple determination of what should or should not be allowed as an estate tax refund. Among the over 1,000 statutes and numerous federal regulations that DOMA controls are laws pertaining to Social Security, housing, taxes, criminal sanctions, copyright, and veterans' benefits.

DOMA's principal effect is to identify a subset of state-sanctioned marriages and make them unequal. The principal purpose is to impose inequality, not for other reasons like governmental efficiency. Responsibilities, as well as rights, enhance the dignity and integrity of the person. And DOMA contrives to deprive some couples married under the laws of their State, but not other couples, of both rights and responsibilities. By creating two contradictory marriage regimes within the same State, DOMA forces same-sex couples to live as married for the purpose of state law but unmarried for the purpose of federal law, thus diminishing the stability and predictability of basic personal relations the State has found it proper to acknowledge and protect. By this dynamic DOMA undermines both the public and private significance of state-sanctioned same-sex marriages; for it tells those couples, and all the world, that their otherwise valid marriages are unworthy of federal recognition. This places same-sex couples in an unstable position of being in a second-tier marriage. The differentiation demeans the couple, whose moral and sexual choices the Constitution protects, see Lawrence v. Texas, and whose relationship the State has sought to dignify. And it humiliates tens of thousands of children now being raised by same-sex couples. The law in question makes it even more difficult for the children to understand the integrity and closeness of their own family and its concord with other families in their community and in their daily lives.

Under DOMA, same-sex married couples have their lives burdened, by reason of government decree, in visible and public ways. By its great reach, DOMA touches many aspects of married and family life, from the mundane to the profound. It prevents same-sex married couples from obtaining government healthcare benefits they would otherwise receive. It deprives them of the Bankruptcy Code's special protections for domestic-support obligations. It forces them to follow a complicated procedure to file their state and federal taxes jointly.

For certain married couples, DOMA's unequal effects are even more serious. The federal penal code makes it a crime to "assaul[t], kidna[p], or murde[r] . . . a member of the immediate family" of "a United States official, a United States judge, [or] a Federal law enforcement officer," with the intent to influence or retaliate against that official. Although a "spouse" qualifies as a member of the officer's "immediate family," DOMA makes this protection inapplicable to same-sex spouses.

DOMA also brings financial harm to children of same-sex couples. It raises the cost of health care for families by taxing health benefits provided by employers to their workers' same-sex spouses. And it denies or reduces benefits allowed to families upon the loss of a spouse and parent, benefits that are an integral part of family security. DOMA divests married same-sex couples of the duties and responsibilities that are an essential part of married life and that they in most cases would be honored to accept were DOMA not in force. For instance, because it is expected that spouses will support each other as they pursue educational opportunities, federal law takes into consideration a spouse's income in calculating a student's federal financial aid eligibility. Same-sex married couples are exempt from this requirement. The same is true with respect to federal ethics rules. Federal executive and agency officials are prohibited from "participat[ing] personally and substantially" in matters as to which they or their spouses have a financial interest. [Under] DOMA, however, these Government-integrity rules do not apply to same-sex spouses. . . .

The liberty protected by the Fifth Amendment's Due Process Clause contains within it the prohibition against denying to any person the equal protection of the laws. While the Fifth Amendment itself withdraws from Government the power to degrade or demean in the way this law does, the equal protection guarantee of the Fourteenth Amendment makes that Fifth Amendment right all the more specific and all the better understood and preserved.

The class to which DOMA directs its restrictions and restraints are those persons who are joined in same-sex marriages made lawful by the State. DOMA singles out a class of persons deemed by a State entitled to recognition and protection to enhance their own liberty. It imposes a disability on the class by refusing to acknowledge a status the State finds to be dignified and proper. DOMA instructs all federal officials, and indeed all persons with whom same-sex couples interact, including their own children, that their marriage is less worthy than the marriages of others. The federal statute is invalid, for no legitimate purpose overcomes the purpose and effect to disparage and to injure those whom the State, by its marriage laws, sought to protect in personhood and dignity. By seeking to displace this protection and treating those persons as living in marriages less

VI. Implied Fundamental Rights

respected than others, the federal statute is in violation of the Fifth Amendment. This opinion and its holding are confined to those lawful marriages.

The judgment of the Court of Appeals for the Second Circuit is affirmed.

It is so ordered.

CHIEF JUSTICE ROBERTS, dissenting.

[While] I disagree with the result to which the majority's analysis leads it in this case, I think it more important to point out that its analysis leads no further. The Court does not have before it, and the logic of its opinion does not decide, the distinct question whether the States, in the exercise of their "historic and essential authority to define the marital relation," may continue to utilize the traditional definition of marriage.

The majority goes out of its way to make this explicit in the penultimate sentence of its opinion. It states that "[t]his opinion and its holding are confined to those lawful marriages"—referring to same-sex marriages that a State has already recognized as a result of the local "community's considered perspective on the historical roots of the institution of marriage and its evolving understanding of the meaning of equality." Justice Scalia believes this is a "'bald, unreasoned disclaime[r].'" In my view, though, the disclaimer is a logical and necessary consequence of the argument the majority has chosen to adopt. The dominant theme of the majority opinion is that the Federal Government's intrusion into an area "central to state domestic relations law applicable to its residents and citizens" is sufficiently "unusual" to set off alarm bells. I think the majority goes off course, as I have said, but it is undeniable that its judgment is based on federalism....

JUSTICE SCALIA, with whom JUSTICE THOMAS joins, and with whom [CHIEF JUSTICE ROBERTS] joins as to Part I, dissenting.

I

[In this portion of his dissent, Justice Scalia argues that the Court lacks jurisdiction over the case. This aspect of the dissent is discussed in Chapter 1 F 2 of this Supplement.]

II ...

B

As I have observed before, the Constitution does not forbid the government to enforce traditional moral and sexual norms. See Lawrence v. Texas (Scalia, J., dissenting). I will not swell the U.S. Reports with restatements of that point. It is enough to say that the Constitution neither requires nor forbids our society to approve of same-sex marriage, much as it neither requires nor forbids us to approve of no-fault divorce, polygamy, or the consumption of alcohol.

However, even setting aside traditional moral disapproval of same-sex marriage (or indeed same-sex sex), there are many perfectly valid—indeed, downright boring—justifying rationales for this legislation. Their existence ought to be the end of this case. For they give the lie to the Court's conclusion that only those with hateful hearts could have voted "aye" on this Act. And more importantly, they serve to make the contents of the legislators' hearts quite irrelevant: "It is a familiar principle of constitutional law that this Court will not strike down an otherwise constitutional statute on the basis of an alleged illicit legislative motive." [United States v. O'Brien, 391 U.S. 524 (1974)]. Or at least it *was* a familiar principle. By holding to the contrary, the majority has declared open season on any law that (in the opinion of the law's opponents and any panel of like-minded federal judges) can be characterized as mean-spirited.

The majority concludes that the only motive for this Act was the "bare . . . desire to harm a politically unpopular group." Bear in mind that the object of this condemnation is not the legislature of some once-Confederate Southern state (familiar objects of the Court's scorn), but our respected coordinate branches, the Congress and Presidency of the United States. Laying such a charge against them should require the most extraordinary evidence, and I would have thought that every attempt would be made to indulge a more anodyne explanation for the statute. . . .

To choose just one of these defenders' arguments, DOMA avoids difficult choice-of-law issues that will now arise absent a uniform federal definition of marriage. . . .

[The] majority says that the supporters of this Act acted with *malice*—with *the "purpose"* "to disparage and to injure" same-sex couples. It says that the motivation for DOMA was to "demean," to "impose inequality," to "impose . . . a stigma," to deny people "equal dignity," to brand gay people as "unworthy and to "*humiliat*[*e*]" their children (emphasis added).

I am sure these accusations are quite untrue. To be sure (as the majority points out), the legislation is called the Defense of Marriage Act. But to defend traditional marriage is not to condemn, demean, or humiliate those who would prefer other arrangements, any more than to defend the Constitution of the United States is to condemn, demean, or humiliate other constitutions. To hurl such accusations so casually demeans *this institution*. In the majority's judgment, any resistance to its holding is beyond the pale of reasoned disagreement. To question its high-handed invalidation of a presumptively valid statute is to act (the majority is sure) with *the purpose* to "disparage," "injure," "degrade," "demean," and "humiliate" our fellow human beings, our fellow citizens, who are homosexual. All that, simply for supporting an Act that did no more than codify an aspect of marriage that had been unquestioned in our society for most of its existence—indeed, had been unquestioned in virtually all societies for virtually all of human history. It is one thing for a society to elect change; it is another for a court of law to impose

VI. Implied Fundamental Rights

change by adjudging those who oppose it *hostes humani generis,* enemies of the human race.

* * *

The penultimate sentence of the majority's opinion is a naked declaration that "[t]his opinion and its holding are confined" to those couples "joined in same-sex marriages made lawful by the State." I have heard such "bald, unreasoned disclaimer[s]" before. [*Lawrence.*] When the Court declared a constitutional right to homosexual sodomy, we were assured that the case had nothing, nothing at all to do with "whether the government must give formal recognition to any relationship that homosexual persons seek to enter." Now we are told that DOMA is invalid because it "demeans the couple, whose moral and sexual choices the Constitution protects,"—with an accompanying citation of *Lawrence.* It takes real cheek for today's majority to assure us, as it is going out the door, that a constitutional requirement to give formal recognition to same-sex marriage is not at issue here—when what has preceded that assurance is a lecture on how superior the majority's moral judgment in favor of same-sex marriage is to the Congress's hateful moral judgment against it. I promise you this: The only thing that will "confine" the Court's holding is its sense of what it can get away with.

I do not mean to suggest disagreement with The Chief Justice's view, that lower federal courts and state courts can distinguish today's case when the issue before them is state denial of marital status to same-sex couples—or even that this Court could *theoretically* do so. Lord, an opinion with such scatter-shot rationales as this one (federalism noises among them) can be distinguished in many ways. And deserves to be. State and lower federal courts should take the Court at its word and distinguish away.

In my opinion, however, the view that *this* Court will take of state prohibition of same-sex marriage is indicated beyond mistaking by today's opinion. As I have said, the real rationale of today's opinion, whatever disappearing trail of its legalistic argle-bargle one chooses to follow, is that DOMA is motivated by "'bare . . . desire to harm'" couples in same-sex marriages. How easy it is, indeed how inevitable, to reach the same conclusion with regard to state laws denying same-sex couples marital status. Consider how easy (inevitable) it is to make the following substitutions in a passage from today's opinion:

> ~~DOMA's~~ *This state law's* principal effect is to identify a subset of ~~state-sanctioned marriages~~ *constitutionally protected sexual relationships,* see *Lawrence,* and make them unequal. The principal purpose is to impose inequality, not for other reasons like governmental efficiency. Responsibilities, as well as rights, enhance the dignity and integrity of the person. And ~~DOMA~~ *this state law* contrives to deprive some couples ~~married under the~~

~~laws of their State~~ *enjoying constitutionally protected sexual relationships,* but not other couples, of both rights and responsibilities. . . .

Similarly transposable passages—deliberately transposable, I think—abound. In sum, that Court which finds it so horrific that Congress irrationally and hatefully robbed same-sex couples of the "personhood and dignity" which state legislatures conferred upon them, will of a certitude be similarly appalled by state legislatures' irrational and hateful failure to acknowledge that "personhood and dignity" in the first place. As far as this Court is concerned, no one should be fooled; it is just a matter of listening and waiting for the other shoe. . . .

[Few] public controversies touch an institution so central to the lives of so many, and few inspire such attendant passion by good people on all sides. Few public controversies will ever demonstrate so vividly the beauty of what our Framers gave us, a gift the Court pawns today to buy its stolen moment in the spotlight: a system of government that permits us to rule *ourselves*. Since DOMA's passage, citizens on all sides of the question have seen victories and they have seen defeats. There have been plebiscites, legislation, persuasion, and loud voices—in other words, democracy. Victories in one place for some, see North Carolina Const., Amdt. 1 (providing that "[m]arriage between one man and one woman is the only domestic legal union that shall be valid or recognized in this State") (approved by a popular vote, 61% to 39% on May 8, 2012), are offset by victories in other places for others, see Maryland Question 6 (establishing "that Maryland's civil marriage laws allow gay and lesbian couples to obtain a civil marriage license") (approved by a popular vote, 52% to 48%, on November 6, 2012). Even in a *single State,* the question has come out differently on different occasions. Compare Maine Question 1 (permitting "the State of Maine to issue marriage licenses to same-sex couples") (approved by a popular vote, 53% to 47%, on November 6, 2012) with Maine Question 1 (rejecting "the new law that lets same-sex couples marry") (approved by a popular vote, 53% to 47%, on November 3, 2009).

In the majority's telling, this story is black-and-white: Hate your neighbor or come along with us. The truth is more complicated. It is hard to admit that one's political opponents are not monsters, especially in a struggle like this one, and the challenge in the end proves more than today's Court can handle. Too bad. A reminder that disagreement over something so fundamental as marriage can still be politically legitimate would have been a fit task for what in earlier times was called the judicial temperament. We might have covered ourselves with honor today, by promising all sides of this debate that it was theirs to settle and that we would respect their resolution. We might have let the People decide.

But that the majority will not do. Some will rejoice in today's decision, and some will despair at it; that is the nature of a controversy that matters so much to

VI. Implied Fundamental Rights

so many. But the Court has cheated both sides, robbing the winners of an honest victory, and the losers of the peace that comes from a fair defeat. We owed both of them better. I dissent.

JUSTICE ALITO, with whom JUSTICE THOMAS joins as to Parts II and III, dissenting. . . .

I

[In this section of his opinion, Justice Alito argues that the case is properly before the Court. This part of the opinion is discussed in Chapter 1 F 2 of this Supplement.]

II . . .

Same-sex marriage presents a highly emotional and important question of public policy—but not a difficult question of constitutional law. The Constitution does not guarantee the right to enter into a same-sex marriage. Indeed, no provision of the Constitution speaks to the issue.

The Court has sometimes found the Due Process Clauses to have a substantive component that guarantees liberties beyond the absence of physical restraint. And the Court's holding that "DOMA is unconstitutional as a deprivation of the liberty of the person protected by the Fifth Amendment of the Constitution," suggests that substantive due process may partially underlie the Court's decision today. But it is well established that any "substantive" component to the Due Process Clause protects only "those fundamental rights and liberties which are, objectively, 'deeply rooted in this Nation's history and tradition,'" Washington v. Glucksberg, as well as "'implicit in the concept of ordered liberty,' such that 'neither liberty nor justice would exist if they were sacrificed.'" *Glucksberg* (quoting Palko v. Connecticut).

It is beyond dispute that the right to same-sex marriage is not deeply rooted in this Nation's history and tradition. In this country, no State permitted same-sex marriage until the Massachusetts Supreme Judicial Court held in 2003 that limiting marriage to opposite-sex couples violated the State Constitution. Nor is the right to same-sex marriage deeply rooted in the traditions of other nations. No country allowed same-sex couples to marry until the Netherlands did so in 2000.

What Windsor and the United States seek, therefore, is not the protection of a deeply rooted right but the recognition of a very new right, and they seek this innovation not from a legislative body elected by the people, but from unelected judges. Faced with such a request, judges have cause for both caution and humility.

The family is an ancient and universal human institution. Family structure reflects the characteristics of a civilization, and changes in family structure and in the popular understanding of marriage and the family can have profound effects. Past changes in the understanding of marriage—for example, the gradual ascendance of the idea that romantic love is a prerequisite to marriage—have had far-reaching consequences. But the process by which such consequences come about is complex, involving the interaction of numerous factors, and tends to occur over an extended period of time.

We can expect something similar to take place if same-sex marriage becomes widely accepted. The long-term consequences of this change are not now known and are unlikely to be ascertainable for some time to come. There are those who think that allowing same-sex marriage will seriously undermine the institution of marriage. Others think that recognition of same-sex marriage will fortify a now-shaky institution.

At present, no one—including social scientists, philosophers, and historians—can predict with any certainty what the long-term ramifications of widespread acceptance of same-sex marriage will be. And judges are certainly not equipped to make such an assessment. The Members of this Court have the authority and the responsibility to interpret and apply the Constitution. Thus, if the Constitution contained a provision guaranteeing the right to marry a person of the same sex, it would be our duty to enforce that right. But the Constitution simply does not speak to the issue of same-sex marriage. In our system of government, ultimate sovereignty rests with the people, and the people have the right to control their own destiny. Any change on a question so fundamental should be made by the people through their elected officials.

III

Perhaps because they cannot show that same-sex marriage is a fundamental right under our Constitution, Windsor and the United States couch their arguments in equal protection terms. They argue that § 3 of DOMA discriminates on the basis of sexual orientation, that classifications based on sexual orientation should trigger a form of "heightened" scrutiny, and that § 3 cannot survive such scrutiny. They further maintain that the governmental interests that § 3 purports to serve are not sufficiently important and that it has not been adequately shown that § 3 serves those interests very well. The Court's holding, too, seems to rest on "the equal protection guarantee of the Fourteenth Amendment,"—although the Court is careful not to adopt most of Windsor's and the United States' argument.

In my view, the approach that Windsor and the United States advocate is misguided. Our equal protection framework, upon which Windsor and the United States rely, is a judicial construct that provides a useful mechanism for analyzing a certain universe of equal protection cases. But that framework is ill suited for use in evaluating the constitutionality of laws based on the traditional understanding of marriage, which fundamentally turn on what marriage is. . . .

VI. Implied Fundamental Rights

In asking the Court to determine that § 3 of DOMA is subject to and violates heightened scrutiny, Windsor and the United States thus ask us to rule that the presence of two members of the opposite sex is as rationally related to marriage as white skin is to voting or a Y-chromosome is to the ability to administer an estate. That is a striking request and one that unelected judges should pause before granting. Acceptance of the argument would cast all those who cling to traditional beliefs about the nature of marriage in the role of bigots or superstitious fools.

By asking the Court to strike down DOMA as not satisfying some form of heightened scrutiny, Windsor and the United States are really seeking to have the Court resolve a debate between two competing views of marriage.

The first and older view, which I will call the "traditional" or "conjugal" view, sees marriage as an intrinsically opposite-sex institution. BLAG notes that virtually every culture, including many not influenced by the Abrahamic religions, has limited marriage to people of the opposite sex. And BLAG attempts to explain this phenomenon by arguing that the institution of marriage was created for the purpose of channeling heterosexual intercourse into a structure that supports child rearing. Others explain the basis for the institution in more philosophical terms. They argue that marriage is essentially the solemnizing of a comprehensive, exclusive, permanent union that is intrinsically ordered to producing new life, even if it does not always do so. While modern cultural changes have weakened the link between marriage and procreation in the popular mind, there is no doubt that, throughout human history and across many cultures, marriage has been viewed as an exclusively opposite-sex institution and as one inextricably linked to procreation and biological kinship.

The other, newer view is what I will call the "consent-based" vision of marriage, a vision that primarily defines marriage as the solemnization of mutual commitment — marked by strong emotional attachment and sexual attraction — between two persons. At least as it applies to heterosexual couples, this view of marriage now plays a very prominent role in the popular understanding of the institution. Indeed, our popular culture is infused with this understanding of marriage. Proponents of same-sex marriage argue that because gender differentiation is not relevant to this vision, the exclusion of same-sex couples from the institution of marriage is rank discrimination.

The Constitution does not codify either of these views of marriage (although I suspect it would have been hard at the time of the adoption of the Constitution or the Fifth Amendment to find Americans who did not take the traditional view for granted). The silence of the Constitution on this question should be enough to end the matter as far as the judiciary is concerned. Yet, Windsor and the United States implicitly ask us to endorse the consent-based view of marriage and to reject the traditional view, thereby arrogating to ourselves the power to decide a question that philosophers, historians, social scientists, and theologians are better qualified to explore. Because our constitutional order assigns the resolution of questions of this nature to the people, I would not presume to enshrine either vision of marriage in our constitutional jurisprudence. . . .

To the extent that the Court takes the position that the question of same-sex marriage should be resolved primarily at the state level, I wholeheartedly agree. I hope that the Court will ultimately permit the people of each State to decide this question for themselves. Unless the Court is willing to allow this to occur, the whiffs of federalism in the today's opinion of the Court will soon be scattered to the wind.

In any event, § 3 of DOMA, in my view, does not encroach on the prerogatives of the States, assuming of course that the many federal statutes affected by DOMA have not already done so. Section 3 does not prevent any State from recognizing same-sex marriage or from extending to same-sex couples any right, privilege, benefit, or obligation stemming from state law. All that § 3 does is to define a class of persons to whom federal law extends certain special benefits and upon whom federal law imposes certain special burdens. In these provisions, Congress used marital status as a way of defining this class—in part, I assume, because it viewed marriage as a valuable institution to be fostered and in part because it viewed married couples as comprising a unique type of economic unit that merits special regulatory treatment. Assuming that Congress has the power under the Constitution to enact the laws affected by § 3, Congress has the power to define the category of persons to whom those laws apply. . . .

H. *The Contracts and Takings Clauses*

Page 1003. At the end of section 3 of the Note, add the following:

Compare Arkansas Game & Fish Commission v. United States, 133 S. Ct. 511 (2012). The Commission owned a wildlife management area along the banks of the Black River, and regularly harvested timber in the reserve as part of its forest management efforts. One hundred fifteen miles upstream from the management area is the Clearwater Dam (the Dam), constructed by the United States Corps of Engineers in 1948. Shortly after constructing the Dam, the Corps adopted a Water Control Manual, which determined the rates at which water would be released from the Dam. In 1993, the Corps approved a planned deviation from the release rate in response to requests from farmers to provide for a longer harvest period. To reduce accumulation of water in the lake behind the Dam, the Corps extended the period in which a high amount of water would be released, resulting in flooding in the management area above historical norms. The flooding resulted in the destruction of timber in the management area and necessitated

VI. Implied Fundamental Rights

costly reclamation measures. Had the Corps released the water at a lower rate, the farmers would have had a shorter harvest season, but the timber would not have been damaged. The Court, in a unanimous decision written by Justice Ginsburg, held that government-induced flooding can amount to a taking even if it is temporary in duration.

If the Corps had not released the water, the farmers would have had a shorter harvest season. Why wouldn't this have been a taking? Suppose that the management area would have been flooded if the Dam had not been built in the first place. Would release of the extra water still be a taking? Would the result be different if the Corps built the Dam but then tore it down? If the initial Water Control Manual had provided for release of water at the higher rate?

Page 1011. At the end of section 1 of the Note, add the following:

Compare Koontz v. St. Johns River Water Management District, 133 S. Ct. 2586 (2013). Petitioner owned a parcel of land that required state permits in order to develop. Petitioner suggested certain limitations on the development to mitigate the environmental damage, but the state Water Management District found these insufficient. Instead, the District proposed that petitioner either take further measures to mitigate the damage on his own property or that he hire contractors to make improvements on other property owned by the District. Petitioner refused to take these measures, and the District denied petitioner's application. Relying upon *Nollan,* Petitioner then filed suit in state court, but the Florida Supreme Court held that *Nollan* was distinguishable because there the state had approved an application on the condition that the land owner acceded to the state's demands, whereas here, the state had denied the application because he refused to make the concessions.

The United States Supreme Court, in a five-to-four decision, rejected this distinction and reversed the judgment below. Writing for the Court, Justice Alito stated that the principles undergirding *Nollan* "do not change depending on whether the government *approves* a permit on the condition that the applicant turn over property or *denies* a permit because the applicant refuses to do so. We have often concluded that denials of governmental benefits were impermissible under the unconstitutional conditions doctrine."

Neither party disputed the proposition that the District could have simply refused to grant the permit. How was petitioner made worse off by the District's suggestion of actions petitioner could take that would lead it to grant the permit? Consider in this regard Justice Alito's observation that "land-use permit applicants are especially vulnerable to the type of coercion that the unconstitutional conditions doctrine prohibits because the government often has broad discretion to deny a permit that is worth far more than property it would like to take." Compare the following observations in Justice Kagan's dissenting opinion:

> Consider the matter from the standpoint of the District's lawyer. The District, she learns, has found that [petitioner's] permit applications do not satisfy legal requirements. It can deny the permits on that basis; or it can suggest ways for [petitioner] to bring his application into compliance. If every suggestion could become the subject of a lawsuit under *Nollan,* [the] lawyer can give but one recommendation: Deny the permits without giving [petitioner] any advice—even if he asks for guidance. [Nothing] in the Takings Clause requires that folly.

Page 1011. At the end of section 2 of the Note, add the following:

Suppose instead of demanding a property interest to which it was otherwise not entitled, the state simply demands cash in return for a permit application. As noted above, in Koontz v. St. Johns River Water Management District, 133 S. Ct. 2586 (2013), the District offered to allow petitioner to proceed with development if petitioner paid for improvements on a different parcel owned by the District. The Florida Supreme Court held that this situation was not governed by *Nollan* and *Dolan* because the requirement of a monetary payment did not constitute a "taking."

In his opinion for a five-to-four majority, Justice Alito rejected this reasoning: "[If] we accepted this argument it would be very easy for land-use permitting officials to evade the limitations of *Nollan* and *Dolan*. Because the government need only provide a permit applicant with one alternative that satisfies the nexus and rough proportionality standards, a permitting authority wishing to exact an easement could simply give the owner a choice of either surrendering an easement or making a payment equal to the easement's value."

The Court recognized that the takings clause does not apply to government-imposed financial obligations that do not operate upon or alter an identified property interest. Here, however, it found that the demand for money did operate upon such an interest "by directing the owner of a particular piece of property to make a monetary payment." The monetary obligation therefore "burdened petitioner's ownership of a specific parcel of land."

The Court acknowledged that neither a requirement that petitioner pay money to the state when not associated with a permit application nor the outright denial of a permit application would constitute a taking. How, then, can putting petitioner

VI. Implied Fundamental Rights — Page 1013

to a choice between these two options be a taking? Compare Rumsfeld v. FAIR, 547 U.S. 47 (2006), discussed in the main volume at page 1417. A federal statute provided that if a university denied access to military recruiters, it would lose access to federal funds. The Court, in a unanimous opinion written by Chief Justice Roberts, upheld the amendment on the ground that universities did not have a constitutional right either to the federal funds or to exclude the military. Are *Rumsfeld* and *Koontz* consistent?

Page 1013. At the end of section 4 of the Note, add the following:

Compare Arkansas Game & Fish Commission v. United States, 133 S. Ct. 511 (2012), where the Court, in a unanimous decision by Justice Ginsburg, held that government action producing temporary flooding of property can constitute a compensable taking. Although the Court held that there was "no automatic exemption from Takings Clause inspection," it also noted that whether there was in fact a taking depended on factors like the length of time that the area was flooded, the degree to which the invasion was intended or foreseeable, the character of the land, and the owner's reasonable investment-backed expectations regarding the land's use.

VII
FREEDOM OF EXPRESSION

A. Introduction

Page 1035. After section d of the Note, add the following:

e. R. Collins & D. Skover, On Dissent: Its Meaning in America 103, 115-116 (2013):

[The First Amendment] safeguards the speech of those who refute our creeds, reject our values, renounce our government, and even repudiate our very way of life. This uniquely American principle of free speech provides a haven for irritating ranters and irksome rogues who feel the need to spoil our parade. In short, it protects the voice of the other. [In] one way or the other, the idea of dissent finds followers in every ideological camp. [As] Benjamin Franklin observed, "[i]t is the first responsibility of every citizen to question authority." [The] First Amendment sometimes converts illegal action into lawful action; it transforms what was seen as anarchy into what may be viewed as democratic engagement; and it reconfigures the relationship between society and its critics.

B. Content-Based Restrictions: Dangerous Ideas and Information

Page 1052. At the end of section 2 of the Note, add the following:

T. Healy, The Great Dissent: How Oliver Wendell Holmes Changed His Mind—and Changed the History of Free Speech in America 201, 343 (2013), provides a full account of Holmes's transformation. It began with a chance encounter with Learned Hand on a train in the summer of 1919. In the following months, Holmes came "under considerable pressure to rethink" his position. His opinions in *Schenck, Frohwerk,* and *Debs* were "attacked in the pages of the New Republic" by University of Chicago law professor Ernst Freund and in "the Harvard Law Review, challenged in correspondence with Learned Hand, confronted over tea by [Harvard law professor] Zechariah Chafee." The political theorist Harold Laski "fed him one book after another espousing a liberal view of free speech," and a young Felix Frankfurter "tried to arrange for him to write a piece on tolerance in the Atlantic Monthly." Although initially resistant to the criticism, Holmes came around. In 1922, Holmes confessed in a letter to Chafee that before the summer of 1919, when it came to issues of free speech and tolerance, "I was simply ignorant."

Page 1053. After section 5 of the Note, add the following:

5a. *"Sentences of twenty years imprisonment."* Holmes is clearly appalled that the defendants in *Abrams* were sentenced to terms "of twenty years imprisonment." He implies that the only plausible explanation for such severe punishment is that the defendants were being "made to suffer" not for any actual harm they might have caused to the nation (which he regards as trivial), but because of the government's hostility to their ideas (which he regards as impermissible). Suppose, then, that the defendants had been sentenced to a fine of $100 instead of to twenty years in prison. Should that have changed Holmes's analysis or the result? Should the nature or severity of the penalty be relevant to the constitutionality of a restriction of speech? See Coenen, Of Speech and Sanctions: Toward a Penalty-Sensitive Approach to the First Amendment, 112 Colum. L. Rev. 991 (2012).

Page 1070. After the long quotation from the opinion in *Yates*, add the following:

Harlan's opinion in *Yates* was greeted with puzzlement. One newspaper at the time characterized it as "a masterpiece of hair-splitting" and scholars characterized it as "complex, scholarly, and painfully dull" and as "a sort of *Finnegan's Wake* of impossibly nice distinctions." Nonetheless, "the Justice Department, faced with *Yates*'s insistence upon proof of advocacy to '*do* something, now or in the future, rather than merely to *believe* in something,' soon admitted that 'we cannot satisfy the evidentiary requirements laid down by the Supreme Court' and dismissed" all remaining Smith Act conspiracy cases then pending. R. Lichtman,

The Supreme Court and McCarthy Era Repression: One Hundred Decisions 95-96 (2012).

Page 1078. Before the Note, add the following:

Consider Tarkington, A First Amendment Theory for Protecting Attorney Speech, 45 U.C. Davis L. Rev. 27, 79 (2011):

The "material support" statute in *Humanitarian Law Project* not only *frustrates* the attorney-client relationship [but] in fact *criminalizes* [it] and imputes culpability for the client's unlawful conduct onto the advising attorney. As with Red Scare statutes aimed at eradicating communism, the "material support" statute, as applied to the plaintiffs, can be said to "quite literally establish[ ] guilt by association alone" because it criminalizes association even if the associating attorney "disagree[s] with th[e] unlawful aims of the [organization]."

Consider also L. Tribe & J. Matz, Uncertain Justice: The Roberts Court and the Constitution 131 (2014): "As the landmark Roberts Court case about free speech in wartime, HLP sends a clear signal: judges must defer, and then defer again, to government when it seeks to justify bans on speech. So long as the 'informed judgment' of the government, some fact-finding on the general subject, and abstract reasoning all support the censorship as a tool against terrorism, it may well survive review. [As] as result, HLP will likely marginalize the Judiciary in protecting free speech in the national security field for many years to come."

Page 1100. At the end of *Snyder v. Phelps*, add the following:

Suppose a gay teenager dies in a car accident and the members of the Westboro Baptist Church picket his funeral. Suppose further that their speech is directed specifically at the parents of the boy, rather than at the general public. Their signs charge that the son died because he was gay, condemn the parents for failing to "correct" their son's homosexuality, and blame them for his death. Would the case be any different? See Heyman, To Drink the Cup of Fury: Funeral Picketing, Public Discourse, and the First Amendment, 45 Conn. L. Rev. 101 (2012). In the years since *Snyder*, many states have enacted "buffer-zone" laws that prohibit any picketing within a certain distance of a funeral within a certain time before and after the funeral. Are such laws constitutional? See Heyman, supra, at 164-172.

Page 1112. At the end of section 7 of the Note, add the following:

7a. *Snowden.* If Edward Snowden returns to the United States, could he be prosecuted and convicted, consistent with the First Amendment, for disclosing to journalists and thus to the world massive amounts of classified information about previously secret NSA surveillance programs? Consider the following positions:

a. Snowden accepted a position of trust in his relation to the government. He did not have to accept his job, but he did. A clear condition of that job was his voluntary agreement not to disclose any *classified* information. That agreement is binding. Period.
b. An individual government employee should never have the authority, on his own say, to override the judgments of the elected representatives of the American people and to decide for the nation that classified information should be disclosed to friends and foes alike. The question is *who* gets to decide when classified information should be made public. It should not be any Tom, Dick and Harry government employee or private contractor with a security clearance who thinks he knows better than the President, the Congress, and the courts about how best to protect the nation's security.
c. Suppose the disclosure of the previously secret programs renders them ineffective in the future, thus seriously damaging the nation's ability to ferret out possible terrorist plots. Should Snowden nonetheless have a First Amendment defense if, upon learning about the previously secret programs, the public opposes them as a matter of policy? If the programs are found to have been illegal? If some of the programs he disclosed were illegal and others were legal?
d. Does your view on any of these positions change if the prosecution is directed against the newspaper publishing Snowden's revelations rather than against Snowden himself?

Page 1112. After section 8 of the Note, add the following:

9. *Facts and the First Amendment.* Note that in many cases the government is attempting to restrict the dissemination of facts rather than opinions. The seminal conception of the First Amendment was about the "marketplace of ideas." How do facts fit into this marketplace? Should government efforts to restrict the dissemination of facts be treated the same way as government efforts to restrict the dissemination of ideas? In addition to the cases in this section, consider also the following: (a) an anti-abortion group publishes on its website the names and addresses of abortion providers; (b) a newspaper publishes the name of a rape victim;

(c) a reporter discloses the names of covert American agents in Iran. See Bhagwat, Details: Specific Facts and the First Amendment, 86 S. Cal. L. Rev. 1 (2012).

D. Content-Based Restrictions: "Low" Value

Page 1142. Before section 5 of the Note, add the following:

e. Kendrick, Speech, Intent, and the Chilling Effect, 54 Wm. & Mary L. Rev. 1633 (2013):
The chilling-effect account holds some appeal. [But] there are reasons to doubt [it]. An argument based on the chilling effect necessarily rests on suppositions about the deterrent effects of law. These suppositions in turn rest upon predictions about the behavior of speakers under counterfactual conditions. Meanwhile, the selection of a remedy, such as an intent requirement, rests on similar predictions about the remedy's speech-protective effects. In short, both the detection of a problem and the imposition of a remedy rest upon intractable empirical suppositions. [In fact], the chilling effect provides at best a weak justification for existing intent requirements in First Amendment law. [Although] at first blush these requirements might seem acceptable as a matter of rough empirical surmise, in reality they often fail to persuade.

Page 1149. At the end of section c of the Note, add the following:

Ashdown, Distorting Democracy: Campaign Lies in the 21st Century, 20 Wm. & Mary Bill Rts. J. 1085 (2012).

Page 1153. Before *Hustler*, add the following:

Consider Norton, Lies and the Constitution, 2012 Sup. Ct. Rev. 161, 169, 185-187, 200:
Unless we are willing to protect all lies or no lies from government regulation, we must make some difficult judgments in determining when the Constitution permits government to punish intentional falsehoods. [Both] the Kennedy and Breyer approaches [in *Alvarez*] defined that core area largely in terms of harm.
[To] this end, we might usefully separate the second- and third-party harms of lies when thinking about whether and when such harms should justify government intervention. [Some lies] harm second parties—that is, the listeners to whom the lie is told. [Examples range from] fraudulent lies that cause monetary harm to

cruel lies that cause emotional harm. Lies can also harm individual third parties (i.e., someone other than the listener)—as is the case with defamation, where the harm is generally suffered not by the listeners but by the subject of the lie. Third-party harms can [also] include more generalized harms to government institutions when, for example, lies undermine the public's confidence in important government processes. [Examples would include perjury at a trial, misrepresenting oneself as a police officer, and a candidate's lies about his credentials]. ...

The great number and variety of lies [undermine] efforts to characterize all—or none—as fully protected by the First Amendment. This requires us to draw some uncomfortable distinctions. [We] can better assess the potential harm of [lies] when we understand them [as threatening either] second-party harms to listeners [or] as third-party harms to the public trust.

Page 1173. At the end of section 1c of the Note, add the following:

Consider also Stone, Ronald Coase's First Amendment, 54 J. Law & Econ. 367, 374 (2011):

> As both logic and history teach, the temptation of public officials to use government power to stifle criticism and distort public debate poses a direct threat to the very existence of a self-governing society. Such behavior not only gives those in power a continuing political advantage over their challengers but also enables them to prevent any criticism or even discussion of their actions. It therefore freezes policies in place. In the sphere of economic regulation, however, that is not the case. As long as free speech is guaranteed, even an inefficient and rent-seeking economic regulation can be publicly criticized and ultimately changed. From a constitutional standpoint, economic freedom simply does not stand on the same footing as freedom of speech.

Page 1173. After section 1e of the Note, add the following:

f. Brudney, The First Amendment and Commercial Advertising, 53 B.C. L. Rev. 1153, 1179, 1168 (2013):

> It has been suggested that because it is speech and serves a communicative function, commercial speech is entitled to the same protection against government regulation as other protected [speech]. As a predicate for First Amendment protection, however, commercial speech's communicative function may not be sufficient to justify such protection. ...

VII. Freedom of Expression   Page 1180

> [This is so because,] in much commercial speech, the speaker's concern is primarily, or only, with the choices to be made by individual consumers for their personal benefit, rather than for the benefit of society as a whole. The question that each consumer is presumed to ask in making his choice is: "What is good, or best, for me?" [But in the case of traditionally protected speech,] the question the addressee or member of the audience is presumed to ask is: "What is good, or best, for the community or society?" Such an inquiry is not of central concern to the speaker-seller or indeed to the listener-buyer [in the context of commercial speech]. . . .

Page 1180. At the end of section 3 of the Note, add the following:

Is the Court's concern with paternalism in these cases warranted? Consider Brudney, The First Amendment and Commercial Speech, 53 B.C. L. Rev. 1153, 1194-1197 (2013):

> Prohibiting or regulating truthful commercial communications about lawful activities that may be of interest to the listener is said to be especially objectionable interference, in that it paternalistically precludes the listener from knowledgeably deciding whether to risk or incur such harm. [In effect, such paternalism interferes with the consumer's ability to make] a possibly harmful choice to satisfy a preference in personal matters [because] the government believes satisfying that preference to be harmful to him or her, as well as to others. . . .
>
> The predicate on which the charge of paternalism rests (the consumers' ability to "perceive their own best interests . . . if they are well enough informed," and to act upon that perception) assumes an apperceptive base of relevant information and knowledge. In the universe of retail mass marketing, the billions of dollars spent by sellers in the aggregate to acculturate consumers to desire products or services that may (or may not) create unspecified long-term health or safety problems, or other costs, are expenditures that are not offset (and are not likely to be offset without government regulation) by reasonably comparable nongovernmental expenditures for educative "debiasing" efforts.
>
> It is that background, structured by government-created property rules in a market economy, that enables sellers or offerors to shape consumer tastes and preferences so as to affect a consumer's "free" choice in responding to offers. It also raises the question: Which government intervention is, or would be, "paternalistic?" Was the consumer's relevant knowledge for making a choice enhanced by the Court's constitutionally rejecting

Virginia's prohibition of price advertisements for prescription drugs? Or was it enhanced by Virginia forbidding such ads? Either way, the government's intervention to enable the consumer "freely" to determine her own best interests is (or is not) "paternalism."

Page 1192. At the end of section 6 of the Note, add the following:

Even if *Stanley* is limited to the home, might the Court's decision in *Lawrence v. Texas* (page 922 of the main volume) suggest that there is a substantive due process right of sexual privacy that, wholly apart from the First Amendment, guarantees the right to purchase and to view obscene expression? See Kinsley, Sexual Privacy in the Internet Age: How Substantive Due Process Protects Online Obscenity, 16 Vand. J. Ent. & Tech. L. 103 (2013). See also Reliable Consultants, Inc. v. Earle, 517 F.3d 738 (5th Cir. 2008) (invalidating a Texas law prohibiting the sale of sexual devices on substantive due process grounds).

Page 1201. After section 9 of the Note, add the following:

10. *Obscenity and substantive due process*. Even if obscenity is not protected by the First Amendment, is it protected from prohibition by the doctrine of substantive due process, as articulated in such decisions as *Griswold v. Connecticut, Roe v. Wade, Planned Parenthood v. Casey,* and *Lawrence v. Texas,* supra section VI F? In *Lawrence*, the Court observed that "liberty gives substantial protection to adult persons in deciding how to conduct their private lives in matters pertaining to sex." Does "the right of autonomous decision-making" in private matters include "the protection of both intimate sexual conduct and the commercial transactions that enable and promote sexual intimacy"? Kinsley, Sexual Privacy in the Internet Age: How Substantive Due Process Protects Online Obscenity, 16 Vand. J. Ent. & Tech. L. 103 (2013). See Reliable Consultants, Inc. v. Earle, 517 F.3d 738 (5th Cir. 2008) (invalidating on substantive due process grounds a Texas law prohibiting any person to sell, advertise, give away or lend any device "designed or marketed for sexual stimulation").

Page 1211. At the end of *United States v. Stevens*, add the following:

Within months of the Supreme Court's decision in *Stevens,* Congress amended § 48. The new provision, titled "Animal crush videos," defines an "animal crush

VII. Freedom of Expression Page 1263

video" as "any photograph, motion-picture film, video or digital recording, or electronic image" that (1) "depicts actual conduct in which one or more living non-human mammals, birds, reptiles, or amphibians is intentionally crushed, burned, drowned, suffocated, impaled or otherwise subjected to serious bodily injury" and (2) "is obscene." The statute exempts any visual depiction of "customary and normal veterinary or agricultural husbandry practices," "the slaughter of animals for food," or "hunting, trapping or fishing." Is this statute constitutional? See United States v. Richards, ___ F. Supp. ___ (S.D. Tex. 2013) (holding that the revised statute violates the First Amendment).

Page 1214. At the end of *Brown v. Entertainment Merchants Association*, add the following:

Consider Schauer, Harm(s) and the First Amendment, 2011 Sup. Ct. Rev. 81, 108, 110:

> *Stevens, Snyder,* and *Entertainment Merchants* all involved moderately clear harms—to animals, to grieving parents, and [to] potential victims of the aggressiveness of teenagers. [The] First Amendment, as much if not more than the rest of the Constitution, is a mandate to the courts to engage in a common law process of developing the rules, principles, standards, maxims, canons, and precedents that together produce what we call legal doctrine. But in considering the common law nature of that development of First Amendment doctrine, it is important to bear in mind Lord Mansfield's optimistic assessment that the common law "works itself pure." In light of [this] aspiration, it is often appropriate to ask whether the progression of time, the increase in the stock of examples, and the continued testing of provisional rules and principles has produced improvement. . . .

Do you agree with Schauer that "one of the surprising things about *Stevens, Snyder,* and *Entertainment Merchants,* taken as a group, is that they give little cause for optimism about the continuing refinement of First Amendment doctrine"?

E. *Content-Neutral Restrictions*

Page 1263. At the end of the Note, add the following:

How has the Roberts Court interpreted and applied the *Chaplinsky* dictum? In the decades after *Chaplinsky,* defenders of free speech viewed the *Chaplinsky*

Page 1263   **VII. Freedom of Expression**

dictum as an "unfortunate" invitation to the Court to make open-ended value judgments about which speech is and is not to be protected by the First Amendment. Indeed, Harry Kalven criticized it in the early 1970s as a "broad dictum" that "haunted constitutional law." H. Kalven, A Worthy Tradition: Freedom of Speech in America 18 (1988). In light of the Roberts Court's decisions in *Stevens, Snyder, Brown,* and *Alvarez,* however, the *Chaplinsky* dictum seems to have taken on a somewhat different cast. Consider Collins, Exceptional Freedom: The Roberts Court, the First Amendment, and the New Absolutism, 76 Alb. L. Rev. 409, 424 (2013):

> [The Roberts Court] has shown no signs of moving away from the jurisprudence of its predecessors in diminishing the domain of *Chaplinsky*'s original exceptions. (For example, pre-Roberts Courts have held that defamation is not entirely unprotected, and lewd and profane speech is sometimes protected.) Moreover, the current Court has generally declined to expressly invoke *Chaplinsky*'s low value [doctrine] as a rationale for enlarging the realm of unprotected expression. In fact, the Court seems to have moved in the opposite direction. [While] some earlier Courts relied on *Chaplinsky*'s two-level theory to cabin free speech protection [citing *Roth*], the Roberts Court has sometimes taken an entirely different approach, one that expands the domain of protected speech. In doing so, it has produced an exceptional kind of freedom in which [speech is] categorically protected unless [it is] among the designated kinds of expression definitely exempted from First Amendment protection.

Page 1274. At the end of the Note, add the following:

    6. *Content or not?* In McCullen v. Coakley, 134 S. Ct. 2518 (2014), the Supreme Court considered the constitutionality of a Massachusetts statute that made it a crime for any person knowingly to stand on a "public way or sidewalk" within 35 feet of an entrance or driveway to any place, other than a hospital, where abortions are performed. The law was designed to eliminate clashes between abortion opponents and advocates of abortion rights that had occurred outside clinics where abortions were performed. The law was challenged by individuals "who approach and talk to women outside such facilities, attempting to dissuade them from having abortions." According to testimony presented at the trial, such individuals have, over time, "persuaded hundreds of women to forgo abortions." The Act exempted persons entering or leaving the facility, employees or agents of the facility, law enforcement and similar personnel, and persons using the sidewalk area solely for the purpose of reaching another destination. The Court, in an

opinion by Chief Justice Roberts, invalidated the law as an unconstitutional content-neutral restriction of speech in a traditional public forum. See insert in this Supplement for page 1281 of the main volume.

The challengers also argued, however, that the law was an unconstitutional content-based restriction of speech, because it applied only at facilities that performed abortions and therefore had a disparate impact on those who oppose abortion. Chief Justice Roberts rejected this argument: "To begin, the Act does not draw content based distinctions on its face. The Act would be content based if it required 'enforcement authorities' to 'examine the content of the message that is conveyed to determine whether' a violation has occurred. But it does not. Whether petitioners violate the Act 'depends' not 'on what they say,' but simply on where they say it. Indeed, petitioners can violate the Act merely by standing in a buffer zone, without displaying a sign or uttering a word.

"It is true, of course, that by limiting the buffer zones to abortion clinics, the Act has the 'inevitable effect' of restricting abortion-related speech more than speech on other subjects. But a facially-neutral law does not become content based simply because it may disproportionately affect speech on certain topics. [The] question in such a case is whether the law is 'justified without reference to the content of the regulated speech.' [The] Massachusetts Act is. Its stated purpose is to 'increase public safety at reproductive health care facilities.' [Obstructed] access and congested sidewalks are problems no matter what caused them. A group of individuals can obstruct clinic access and clog sidewalks just as much when they loiter as when they protest abortion or counsel patients. . . . [The challengers argue, however, that] by choosing to pursue these interests only at abortion clinics, [the] Massachusetts Legislature evinced a purpose to 'single[ ] out for regulation speech about one particular topic: abortion.' We cannot infer such a purpose from the Act's limited scope. [The] Massachusetts Legislature [enacted the statute] in response to a problem that was, in its experience, limited to abortion clinics. There was a record of crowding, obstruction, and even violence outside such clinics. There were apparently no similar recurring problems associated with other kinds of healthcare facilities [or other kinds of buildings or activities]. In light of the limited nature of the problem, it was reasonable for the Massachusetts Legislature to enact a limited solution. [W]e thus conclude that the Act is neither content nor viewpoint based and therefore need not be analyzed under strict scrutiny."

Justice Scalia, joined by Justices Kennedy and Thomas, filed a concurring opinion in which he maintained that the challenged statute "is content based and fails strict scrutiny": "[It] blinks reality to say [that] a blanket prohibition on the use of streets and sidewalks where speech on only one politically controversial topic is likely to occur—and where that speech can most effectively be communicated—is not content based. Would the Court exempt from strict scrutiny a law banning access to the streets and sidewalks surrounding the site of the Republican National Convention? Or those used annually to commemorate the 1965 Selma-to-Montgomery civil rights marches? Or those outside the Internal Revenue Service? Surely not. . . .

"The structure of the Act also indicates that it rests on content-based concerns. The goals of 'public safety, patient access to healthcare, and the unobstructed use of public sidewalks and roadways,' are already achieved by an earlier-enacted subsection of the statute. [As] the majority recognizes, that provision is easy to enforce. Thus, the speech-free zones carved out [by the challenged statute] add nothing to safety and access; what they achieve, and what they were obviously designed to achieve, is the suppression of speech opposing abortion. . . .

"In concluding that the statute is content based and therefore subject to strict scrutiny, I necessarily conclude that *Hill v. Colorado* should be overruled. [Protecting] people from speech they do not want to hear is not a function that the First Amendment allows the government to undertake in the public streets and sidewalks."

Justice Alito also filed a concurring opinion: "As the Court recognizes, if the Massachusetts law discriminates on the basis of viewpoint, it is unconstitutional, and I believe the law clearly discriminates on this ground. [The] Massachusetts statute generally prohibits any person from entering a buffer zone around an abortion clinic during the clinic's business hours, but the law contains an exemption for 'employees or agents of such facility acting within the scope of their employment.'

"Thus, during business hours, individuals who wish to counsel against abortion or to criticize the particular clinic may not do so within the buffer zone. If they engage in such conduct, they commit a crime. By contrast, employees and agents of the clinic may enter the zone and engage in any conduct that falls within the scope of their employment. A clinic may direct or authorize an employee or agent, while within the zone, to express favorable views about abortion or the clinic, and if the employee exercises that authority, the employee's conduct is perfectly lawful. In short, petitioners and other critics of a clinic are silenced, while the clinic may authorize its employees to express speech in support of the clinic and its work. [It is thus] clear on the face of the Massachusetts law that it discriminates based on viewpoint. Speech in favor of the clinic and its work by employees and agents is permitted; speech criticizing the clinic and its work is a crime. This is blatant viewpoint discrimination."

VII. Freedom of Expression

Page 1281. Before section 9 of the Note, add the following:

8a. *Demonstrating near an abortion clinic IV.* In McCullen v. Coakley, 134 S. Ct. 2518 (2014), the Supreme Court invalidated a Massachusetts statute that made it a crime for any person knowingly to stand on a "public way or sidewalk" within 35 feet of an entrance or driveway to any place, other than a hospital, where abortions are performed. The law was designed to eliminate clashes between abortion opponents and advocates of abortion rights that had occurred outside clinics where abortions were performed. The law was challenged by individuals "who approach and talk to women outside such facilities, attempting to dissuade them from having abortions." According to testimony presented at the trial, such individuals have, over time, "persuaded hundreds of women to forgo abortions."

Chief Justice Roberts authored the opinion of the Court: "[Public ways and sidewalks] occupy a 'special position in terms of First Amendment protection' because of their historic role as sites for discussion and debate. [Such] traditional public fora are areas that have historically been open to the public for speech activities. [We] have held that the government's ability to restrict speech in such locations is 'very limited.' [Even if such laws are content neutral, they must be] narrowly tailored to serve a significant governmental interest. [For] a content-neutral time, place, or manner regulation to be narrowly tailored, it must not 'burden substantially more speech than is necessary to further the government's legitimate interests.' . . .

"The buffer zones burden substantially more speech than necessary to achieve the Commonwealth's asserted interests. [The] Commonwealth's interests include ensuring public safety outside abortion clinics, preventing harassment and intimidation of patients and clinic staff, and combating deliberate obstruction of clinic entrances. [The Act] itself contains a separate provision [that] prohibits much of this conduct. That provision subjects to criminal punishment '[a]ny person who knowingly obstructs, detains, hinders, impedes or blocks another person's entry to or exit from a reproductive health care facility.' [If] Massachusetts determines that broader prohibitions along the same lines are necessary, it could enact legislation similar to the federal Freedom of Access to Clinic Entrances Act of 1994, which subjects to both criminal and civil penalties anyone who 'by force or threat of force or by physical obstruction, intentionally injures, intimidates or interferes with or attempts to injure, intimidate or interfere with any person because that person is or has been, or in order to intimidate such person or any other person or any class of persons from, obtaining or providing reproductive health services.' [If] the Commonwealth is particularly concerned about harassment, it could also consider an ordinance such as the one adopted in New York City that not only prohibits obstructing access to a clinic, but also makes it a crime 'to follow and harass another person within 15 feet of the premises of a reproductive health care facility.' . . .

"The point is not that Massachusetts must enact all or even any of the proposed measures discussed above. The point is instead that the Commonwealth has available to it a variety of approaches that appear capable of serving its interests without excluding individuals from areas historically open for speech and debate."

Page 1334. At the end of section 3 of the Note, add the following:

Are there circumstances in which the government's own speech might violate the establishment clause? The equal protection clause? See Norton, The Equal Protection Implications of Government's Hateful Speech, 54 Wm. & Mary L. Rev. 159 (2012).

Page 1337. At the end of the Note on Government Speech, add the following:

AGENCY FOR INTERNATIONAL DEVELOPMENT v. ALLIANCE FOR OPEN SOCIETY INTERNATIONAL, 133 S. Ct. 2321 (2013). The United States Leadership Against HIV/AIDS, Tuberculosis, and Malaria Act of 2003 (Leadership Act) authorized the appropriation of billions of dollars to fund efforts by nongovernmental organizations to combat HIV/AIDS worldwide. The Act imposed a condition ("The Policy Requirement") on all recipients of funds under the Act: all recipients must explicitly oppose prostitution. This requirement was challenged by recipients of Leadership Act funds who wish to remain neutral on the issue of prostitution. The Court, in a six-to-two decision, held that this requirement violated the First Amendment rights of recipients.

Chief Justice Roberts delivered the opinion of the Court: "The Policy Requirement mandates that recipients of Leadership Act funds explicitly agree with the Government's policy to oppose prostitution. . . . It is, however, a basic First Amendment principle that 'freedom of speech prohibits the government from telling people what they must say.' [Citing *West Virginia Bd. of Educ. v. Barnette*, main volume page 1416; *Wooley v. Maynard*, main volume page 1416]. [Were The Policy Requirement] enacted as a direct regulation of speech, [it] would plainly violate the First Amendment. The question is whether the Government may nonetheless impose that requirement as a condition on the receipt of federal funds. . . .

"[As] a general matter, if a party objects to a condition on the receipt of federal funding, its recourse is to decline the funds. This remains true when the objection is that a condition may affect the recipient's exercise of its First Amendment rights. [Citing *United States v. American Library Ass'n*.] At the same time, however, we have held that the Government 'may not deny a benefit to a person on a basis that infringes his constitutionally protected . . . freedom of speech even if he has no entitlement to that benefit.' In some cases, a funding condition can result in an unconstitutional burden on First Amendment rights. . . .

"The dissent thinks that can only be true when the condition is not relevant to the objectives of the program [or] when the condition is actually coercive, in the sense of an offer that cannot be refused. Our precedents, however, are not so limited. In the present context, the relevant distinction that has emerged from our cases is between conditions that define the limits of the government spending program—those that specify the activities Congress wants to subsidize—and conditions that seek to leverage funding to regulate speech outside the contours of the program itself. The line is hardly clear, in part because the definition of a particular program can always be manipulated to subsume the challenged condition. We have held, however, that 'Congress cannot recast a condition on funding as a mere definition of its program in every case, lest the First Amendment be reduced to a simple semantic exercise.'" [*Velazquez*.]

As an example, Chief Justice Roberts invoked *FCC v. League of Women Voters*, in which "the Court struck down a condition on federal financial assistance to noncommercial broadcast television and radio stations that prohibited all editorializing, including with private funds. Even a station receiving only one percent of its overall budget from the Federal Government, the Court explained, was 'barred absolutely from all editorializing.' [The] law provided no way for a station to limit its use of federal funds to noneditorializing activities, while using private funds 'to make known its views on matters of public importance.' The prohibition thus went beyond ensuring that federal funds not be used to subsidize 'public broadcasting station editorials,' and instead leveraged the federal funding to regulate the stations' speech outside the scope of the program.

"Our decision in *Rust* elaborated on the approach [in] *League of Women Voters*. In *Rust*, [the] organizations received funds from a variety of sources other than the Federal Government for a variety of purposes. The Act, however, prohibited the Title X federal funds from being 'used in programs where abortion is a method of family planning.' To enforce this provision, HHS regulations barred Title X projects from advocating abortion as a method of family planning, and required grantees to ensure that their Title X projects were 'physically and financially separate' from their other projects that engaged in the prohibited activities. . . .

"We explained that Congress can, without offending the Constitution, selectively fund certain programs to address an issue of public concern, without funding alternative ways of addressing the same problem. In Title X, Congress had defined the federal program to encourage only particular family planning methods. The challenged regulations were simply 'designed to ensure that the limits of the federal program are observed,' and 'that public funds [are] spent for the purposes for which they were authorized.' [The] regulations governed only the scope of the grantee's Title X projects, leaving it 'unfettered in its other activities.' [Title X grantees could continue to engage in abortion advocacy as long as they conducted] 'those activities through programs that are separate and independent from the project that receives Title X funds.' Because the regulations did not 'prohibit[ ] the recipient from engaging in the protected conduct outside the scope of the federally funded program,' they did not run afoul of the First Amendment. Here, however, [the] Policy Requirement falls on the unconstitutional side of the line. [By] demanding that funding recipients adopt—as their own—the Government's view on an issue of public concern, the condition by its very nature affects 'protected conduct outside the scope of the federally funded program.' [By] requiring recipients to profess a specific belief, the Policy Requirement goes beyond defining the limits of the federally funded program to defining the recipient. . . .

"The Government suggests that the Policy Requirement is necessary because, without it, the grant of federal funds could free a recipient's private funds 'to be used to promote prostitution.' [Citing *Holder v. Humanitarian Law Project*.] That argument assumes that federal funding will simply supplant private funding, rather than pay for new programs or expand existing ones. The Government offers no support for that assumption as a general matter, or any reason to believe it is true here. And if the Government's argument were correct, *League of Women Voters* would have come out differently, and much of the reasoning [of] *Rust* would have been beside the point.

"The Government cites but one case to support that argument, *Holder v. Humanitarian Law Project*. That case concerned the quite different context of a ban on providing material support to terrorist organizations, where the record indicated that support for those organizations' nonviolent operations was funneled to support their violent activities.

"Pressing its argument further, the Government contends that 'if organizations awarded federal funds to implement Leadership Act programs could at the same time promote or affirmatively condone prostitution or sex trafficking, whether using public *or private* funds, it would undermine the government's program and confuse its message opposing prostitution.' But the Policy Requirement goes beyond preventing recipients from using private funds in a way that would undermine the federal program. It requires them to pledge allegiance to the Government's policy of eradicating prostitution. As to that, we cannot improve upon what Justice Jackson wrote for the Court 70 years ago: 'If there is any fixed star in our constitutional constellation, it is that no official, high or petty, can prescribe what shall be orthodox in politics, nationalism, religion, or other matters of opinion or force citizens to confess by word or act their faith therein.' [Quoting *West Virginia Bd. of Educ. v. Barnette.*]

"The Policy Requirement compels as a condition of federal funding the affirmation of a belief that by its nature cannot be confined within the scope of the Government program. In so doing, it violates the First Amendment and cannot be sustained."

Justice Scalia, joined by Justice Thomas, dissented: "The First Amendment does not mandate a viewpoint neutral government. Government must choose between rival ideas and adopt some as its own: competition over cartels, solar energy over coal, weapon development over disarmament, and so forth. Moreover, the government may enlist the assistance of those who believe in its ideas to carry them to fruition; and it need not enlist for that purpose those who oppose or do not support the ideas. That seems to me a matter of the most common common sense....

"The argument is that this commonsense principle will enable the government to discriminate against, and injure, points of view to which it is opposed. Of course the Constitution does not prohibit government spending that discriminates against, and injures, points of view to which the government is opposed; every government program which takes a position on a controversial issue does that. Anti-smoking programs injure cigar aficionados, programs encouraging sexual abstinence injure free-love advocates, etc. The constitutional prohibition at issue here is not a prohibition against discriminating against or injuring opposing points of view, but the First Amendment's prohibition against the coercing of speech. I am frankly dubious that a condition for eligibility to participate in a minor federal program such as this one runs afoul of that prohibition even when the condition is irrelevant to the goals of the program. Not every disadvantage is a coercion.

"But that is not the issue before us here. Here the views that the Government demands an applicant forswear—or that the Government insists an applicant favor—are relevant to the program in question. The program is valid only if the Government is entitled to disfavor the opposing view (here, advocacy of or toleration of prostitution). And if the program can disfavor it, so can the selection of those who are to administer the program. There is no risk that this principle will enable the Government to discriminate arbitrarily against positions it disfavors. It would not, for example, permit the Government to exclude from bidding on defense contracts anyone who refuses to abjure prostitution. But here a central part of the Government's HIV/AIDS strategy is the suppression of prostitution, by which HIV is transmitted. It is entirely reasonable to admit to participation in the program only those who believe in that goal....

"Of course the most obvious manner in which the admission to a program of an ideological opponent can frustrate the purpose of the program is by freeing up the opponent's funds for use in its ideological opposition. [Money] is fungible. The economic reality is that when NGOs can conduct their AIDS work on the

Government's dime, they can expend greater resources on policies that undercut the Leadership Act. The Government need not establish by record evidence that this will happen. To make it a valid consideration in determining participation in federal programs, it suffices that this is a real and obvious risk. [In] *FCC v. League of Women Voters,* the ban on editorializing [was] disallowed precisely because it did not further a relevant, permissible policy of the Federal Communications Act. . . .

"The majority cannot credibly say that this speech condition is coercive, so it does not. It pussyfoots around the lack of coercion by invalidating the Leadership Act for '*requiring* recipients to profess a specific belief' and '*demanding* that funding recipients adopt — as their own — the Government's view on an issue of public concern.' But like King Cnut's commanding of the tides, here the Government's 'requiring' and 'demanding' have no coercive effect. In the end, and in the circumstances of this case, [there] is no compulsion at all. It is the reasonable price of admission to a limited government-spending program that each organization remains free to accept or reject. . . ."

Page 1400. Before the Note, add the following:

McCUTCHEON v. FEDERAL ELECTION COMMISSION, 134 S. Ct. 1434 (2014). The federal Bipartisan Campaign Reform Act imposes two types of limits on campaign contributions. The first, called base limits, restricts how much money a donor may contribute to a particular candidate or committee. The second, called aggregate limits, restricts how much money a donor may contribute in total to all candidates or committees. In *Buckley,* the Court upheld the constitutionality of the base contribution limits. This case concerned the constitutionality of the aggregate contribution limits.

For the 2013-2014 election cycle, the aggregate limits permitted an individual to contribute a total of $48,600 to federal candidates and a total of $74,600 to other political committees. In the 2011-2012 election cycle, Shaun McCutcheon contributed a total of $33,088 to sixteen different federal candidates, in compliance with the then-applicable base limits. McCutcheon wanted to contribute $1,776 to each of twelve additional candidates, but was prevented from doing so by the aggregate limit on contributions to candidates. He also wanted to contribute to several additional political committees, including $25,000 to each of the three Republican national party committees, but again was prevented from doing so by the aggregate limit on contributions to political committees. The Republican National Committee wanted to receive the contributions that McCutcheon and other potential contributors wanted to make to it — contributions otherwise permissible under the base limits for national party committees, but foreclosed by the aggregate limit on contributions to political committees.

VII. Freedom of Expression

In June 2012, McCutcheon and the RNC filed a complaint before a three-judge panel of the U.S. District Court for the District of Columbia, maintaining that the aggregate limits on contributions to candidates and to noncandidate political committees were unconstitutional under the First Amendment. The three-judge court dismissed the complaint, holding that the aggregate limits survived First Amendment scrutiny.

The Supreme Court, in a five-to-four decision, held the aggregate contribution limits unconstitutional. Chief Justice Roberts announced the judgment of the Court and delivered an opinion, in which Justices Scalia, Kennedy, and Alito joined:

"The right to participate in democracy through political contributions is protected by the First Amendment, but that right is not absolute. Our cases have held that Congress may regulate campaign contributions to protect against corruption or the appearance of corruption. [Citing *Buckley*.] At the same time, we have made clear that Congress may not regulate contributions simply to reduce the amount of money in politics, or to restrict the political participation of some in order to enhance the relative influence of others. [Citing *Bennett*.] Many people might find those latter objectives attractive. [Money] in politics may at times seem repugnant to some, but so too does much of what the First Amendment vigorously protects. If the First Amendment protects flag burning, funeral protests, and Nazi parades—despite the profound offense such spectacles cause—it surely protects political campaign speech despite popular opposition. . . .

"In a series of cases over the past 40 years, we have spelled out how to draw the constitutional line between the permissible goal of avoiding corruption in the political process and the impermissible desire simply to limit political speech. We have said that government regulation may not target the general gratitude a candidate may feel toward those who support him or his allies, or the political access such support may afford. [Any] regulation must instead target what we have called 'quid pro quo' corruption or its appearance. That Latin phrase captures the notion of a direct exchange of an official act for money. [Campaign] finance restrictions that pursue other objectives . . . impermissibly inject the Government 'into the debate over who should govern.' [Quoting *Bennett*.]

"The statute at issue in this case [restricts] how much money a donor may contribute in total to all candidates or committees. This case does not involve any challenge to the base limits, which we have previously upheld as serving the permissible objective of combatting corruption. The Government contends that the aggregate limits also serve that objective, by preventing circumvention of the base limits. We conclude, however, that the aggregate limits do little, if anything, to address that concern, while seriously restricting participation in the democratic process. The aggregate limits are therefore invalid under the First Amendment. . . .

"The First Amendment 'is designed and intended to remove governmental restraints from the arena of public discussion, putting the decision as to what views shall be voiced largely into the hands of each of us, . . . in the belief that no other approach would comport with the premise of individual dignity and choice upon which our political system rests.' [Quoting *Cohen v. California*.] As relevant here, the First Amendment safeguards an individual's right to participate in the public debate through political expression and political association. When an individual contributes money to a candidate, he exercises both of those rights. [Those] rights are important regardless whether the individual is, on the one hand, a 'lone pamphleteer[ ] or street corner orator' [or] someone who spends 'substantial amounts of money in order to communicate [his] political ideas through sophisticated' means. Either way, he is participating in an electoral debate that we have recognized is 'integral to the operation of the system of government established by our Constitution.' . . .

"To put it in the simplest terms, the aggregate limits prohibit an individual from fully contributing to the campaigns of [all the candidates he wants to support], even if all contributions fall within the base limits Congress views as adequate to protect against corruption. [It] is no answer to say that the individual can simply contribute less money to more people. To require one person to contribute at lower levels than others because he wants to support more candidates or causes is to impose a special burden on broader participation in the democratic process. [The] First Amendment burden is especially great for individuals who do not have ready access to alternative avenues for supporting their preferred politicians and policies. In the context of base contribution limits, *Buckley* observed that a supporter could vindicate his associational interests by personally volunteering his time and energy on behalf of a candidate. Such personal volunteering is not a realistic alternative for those who wish to support a wide variety of candidates or causes. . . .

"With the significant First Amendment costs for individual citizens in mind, we turn to the governmental interests asserted in this case. This Court has identified only one legitimate governmental interest for restricting campaign finances: preventing corruption or the appearance of corruption. We have consistently rejected attempts to suppress campaign speech based on other legislative objectives. No matter how desirable it may seem, it is not an acceptable governmental objective to 'level the playing field,' or to 'level electoral opportunities,' or to 'equaliz[e] the financial resources of candidates.' The First Amendment prohibits such legislative attempts to 'fine-tun[e]' the electoral process, no matter how well intentioned. As we framed the relevant principle in *Buckley*, 'the concept that government may restrict the speech of some elements of our society in order to enhance the relative voice of others is wholly foreign to the First Amendment.' . . .

"Moreover, while preventing corruption or its appearance is a legitimate objective, Congress may target only a specific type of corruption—'quid pro quo'

VII. Freedom of Expression   Page 1400

corruption. [Spending] large sums of money in connection with elections, but not in connection with an effort to control the exercise of an officeholder's official duties, does not give rise to such quid pro quo corruption. Nor does the possibility that an individual who spends large sums may garner 'influence over or access to' elected officials or political parties.

"[The] line between quid pro quo corruption and general influence may seem vague at times, but the distinction must be respected in order to safeguard basic First Amendment rights. . . .

"'When the Government restricts speech, the Government bears the burden of proving the constitutionality of its actions.' Here, the Government seeks to carry that burden by arguing that the aggregate limits further the permissible objective of preventing quid pro quo corruption. The difficulty is that once the aggregate limits kick in, they ban all contributions of any amount. But Congress's selection of a $5,200 base limit indicates its belief that contributions of that amount or less do not create a cognizable risk of corruption. If there is no corruption concern in giving nine candidates up to $5,200 each, it is difficult to understand how a tenth candidate can be regarded as corruptible if given $1,801, and all others corruptible if given a dime. And if there is no risk that additional candidates will be corrupted by donations of up to $5,200, then the Government must defend the aggregate limits by demonstrating that they prevent circumvention of the base limits.

"The problem is that they do not serve that function in any meaningful way. In light of the various statutes and regulations currently in effect, [the] fear that an individual might 'contribute massive amounts of money to a particular candidate through the use of unearmarked contributions' to entities likely to support the candidate, is far too speculative. We 'have never accepted mere conjecture as adequate to carry a First Amendment burden.' [The] primary example of circumvention, in one form or another, envisions an individual donor who contributes the maximum amount under the base limits to a particular candidate, say, Representative Smith. Then the donor also channels 'massive amounts of money' to Smith through a series of contributions to PACs that have stated their intention to support Smith. Various earmarking and antiproliferation rules disarm this example. Importantly, the donor may not contribute to the most obvious PACs: those that support only Smith. Nor may the donor contribute to the slightly less obvious PACs that he knows will route 'a substantial portion' of his contribution to Smith. [Any scheme to funnel huge amounts of money to Smith by indirection, given the restraints already built into the system,] is highly implausible [and] either illegal under current campaign finance laws or divorced from reality. [The] dissent [maintains] that, even with the aggregate limits in place, individuals 'have transferred large sums of money to specific candidates' in excess of the base limits. But the cited sources do not provide any real-world examples of circumvention. . . .

"[Moreover], there are multiple alternatives available to Congress that would serve the Government's anticircumvention interest, while avoiding 'unnecessary

107

abridgment' of First Amendment rights. The most obvious might involve targeted restrictions on transfers among candidates and political committees. There are currently no such limits on transfers among party committees and from candidates to party committees. Perhaps for that reason, a central concern of the District Court [and] the dissent has been the ability of party committees to transfer money freely. If Congress agrees that this is problematic, it might tighten its permissive transfer rules. Doing so would impose a lesser burden on First Amendment rights, as compared to aggregate limits that flatly ban contributions beyond certain levels. [Indeed], Congress has adopted transfer restrictions, and the Court has upheld them, in the context of state party spending. [In addition,] disclosure of contributions minimizes the potential for abuse of the campaign finance system. Disclosure requirements [burden] speech, but—unlike the aggregate limits—they do not impose a ceiling on speech. For that reason, disclosure often represents a less restrictive alternative to flat bans on certain types or quantities of speech. [We] do not mean to opine on the validity of any particular proposal. The point is that there are numerous alternative approaches available to Congress to prevent circumvention of the base limits. . . .

"For the past 40 years, our campaign finance jurisprudence has focused on the need to preserve authority for the Government to combat corruption, without at the same time compromising the political responsiveness at the heart of the democratic process, or allowing the Government to favor some participants in that process over others. [Constituents] have the right to support candidates who share their views and concerns. Representatives are not to follow constituent orders, but can be expected to be cognizant of and responsive to those concerns. Such responsiveness is key to the very concept of self-governance through elected officials. The Government has a strong interest, no less critical to our democratic system, in combatting corruption and its appearance. We have, however, held that this interest must be limited to a specific kind of corruption—quid pro quo corruption—in order to ensure that the Government's efforts do not have the effect of restricting the First Amendment right of citizens to choose who shall govern them. [We] conclude that the aggregate limits on contributions do not further the only governmental interest this Court accepted as legitimate in *Buckley*. They instead intrude without justification on a citizen's ability to exercise 'the most fundamental First Amendment activities.'"

Justice Thomas concurred in the judgment: "I adhere to the view that this Court's decision in *Buckley* denigrates core First Amendment speech and should be overruled.

"[Contributions] to political campaigns, no less than direct expenditures, 'generate essential political speech' by fostering discussion of public issues and candidate qualifications. *Buckley* itself recognized that both contribution and expenditure limits 'operate in an area of the most fundamental First Amendment activities' and 'implicate fundamental First Amendment interests.' But instead of treating political giving and political spending alike, *Buckley* [unjustifiably] distinguished the two, embracing a bifurcated standard of review under which contribution limits receive less rigorous scrutiny. [This] case represents yet another missed opportunity to right the course of our campaign finance jurisprudence by restoring a standard that is faithful to the First Amendment."

Justice Breyer, joined by Justices Ginsburg, Sotomayor, and Kagan, dissented: "Taken together with *Citizens United* [main volume at page 1385], today's decision eviscerates our Nation's campaign finance laws, leaving a remnant incapable of dealing with the grave problems of democratic legitimacy that those laws were intended to resolve. [The] plurality's conclusion rests upon three separate but related claims. Each is fatally flawed. First, the plurality says that given the base limits on contributions to candidates and political committees, aggregate limits do not further any independent governmental objective worthy of protection. And that is because, given the base limits, '[s]pending large sums of money in connection with elections' does not 'give rise to . . . corruption.' In making this argument, the plurality relies heavily upon a narrow definition of 'corruption' that excludes efforts to obtain 'influence over or access to' elected officials or political parties. Second, the plurality assesses the instrumental objective of the aggregate limits, namely, safeguarding the base limits. It finds that they 'do not serve that function in any meaningful way.' That is because, even without the aggregate limits, the possibilities for circumventing the base limits are 'implausible' and 'divorced from reality.' Third, the plurality says the aggregate limits are 'poorly tailored to the Government's interest in preventing circumvention of the base limits.' The plurality imagines several alternative regulations that it says might just as effectively thwart circumvention. Accordingly, it finds, the aggregate caps are out of 'proportion to the [anticorruption] interest served.' . . .

"The plurality's first claim—that large aggregate contributions do not 'give rise' to 'corruption'—is plausible only because the plurality defines 'corruption' too narrowly. [Its] definition of 'corruption' is inconsistent with the Court's prior case law (with the possible exception of *Citizens United*) [and] it misunderstands the constitutional importance of the interests at stake. [The] history of campaign finance reform shows [that] the anticorruption interest that drives Congress to regulate campaign contributions is a far broader, more important interest than the plurality acknowledges. It is an interest in maintaining the integrity of our public governmental institutions. And it is an interest rooted in the Constitution and in the First Amendment itself. [Speech] does not exist in a vacuum. Rather, political communication seeks to secure government action. A politically oriented 'marketplace of ideas' seeks to form a public opinion that can and will influence elected representatives. This is not a new idea. [Citing *Whitney v. California* (Brandeis, J., concurring).] [Accordingly], the First Amendment advances not only the individual's right to engage in political speech, but also the public's interest in preserving a democratic order in which collective speech matters.

"What has this to do with corruption? It has everything to do with corruption. Corruption breaks the constitutionally necessary 'chain of communication' between the people and their representatives. [Where] enough money calls the tune, the general public will not be heard. Insofar as corruption cuts the link between political thought and political action, a free marketplace of political ideas loses its point. [The] 'appearance of corruption' can make matters worse. It can lead the public to believe that its efforts to communicate with its representatives or to help sway public opinion have little purpose. And a cynical public can lose interest in political participation altogether. The upshot is that the interests the Court has long described as preventing 'corruption' or the 'appearance of corruption' are more than ordinary factors to be weighed against the constitutional right to political speech. Rather, they are interests rooted in the First Amendment itself. They are rooted in the constitutional effort to create a democracy responsive to the people—a government where laws reflect the very thoughts, views, ideas, and sentiments, the expression of which the First Amendment protects. Given that end, we can and should understand campaign finance laws as resting upon a broader and more significant constitutional rationale than the plurality's limited definition of 'corruption' suggests. We should see these laws as seeking in significant part to strengthen, rather than weaken, the First Amendment. To say this is not to deny the potential for conflict between (1) the need to permit contributions that pay for the diffusion of ideas, and (2) the need to limit payments in order to help maintain the integrity of the electoral process. But that conflict takes place within, not outside, the First Amendment's boundaries. . . .

"The plurality invalidates the aggregate contribution limits for a second reason. It believes they are no longer needed to prevent contributors from circumventing federal limits on direct contributions to individuals, political parties, and political action committees. [The] plurality is wrong. Here, as in *Buckley*, in the absence of limits on aggregate political contributions, donors can and likely will find ways to channel millions of dollars to parties and to individual candidates, [producing] 'corruption' or 'appearance of corruption.' The methods for using today's opinion to evade the law's individual contribution limits are complex, but they are well known, or will become well known, to party fundraisers. [Justice Breyer then described three such methods in detail.] The plurality believes that the three scenarios I have just depicted either pose no threat, or cannot or will not take place. Not so. [Justice Breyer then explained in detail why, in his view, the absence of aggregate contribution limits will, in fact, enable substantial circumvention of the base contribution limits.] . . .

"The plurality [substitutes its limited understanding] of how the political process works for the understanding of Congress, [and in so doing it] creates huge

VII. Freedom of Expression

loopholes in the law [and] undermines, perhaps devastates, what remains of campaign finance reform."

* * *

Consider the following views:

a. Hellman, Defining Corruption and Constitutionalizing Democracy, 111 Mich. L. Rev. 1385 (2013):

"The main front in the battle over the constitutionality of campaign finance laws has long focused on defining corruption. [But] corruption is a derivative concept, meaning it depends on a theory of the institution or official involved. [What] constitutes corruption in a democracy depends on a theory of democracy. To put the point in a more grounded fashion, what constitutes corruption of legislators depends on a view of the proper basis for decisionmaking by elected officials. [Our] campaign finance case law contains at least three distinct conceptions of legislative corruption. I call these 'corruption as the deformation of judgment,' 'corruption as the distortion of influence,' and 'corruption as the sale of favors.' . . .

On one view, a legislator ought to exercise his own independent judgment about each decision he faces. [The] legislator, according to this view, should consider only the merits-based reasons that bear on the decision at hand. [Corruption as the "deformation of judgment"] occurs when non-merits-based factors influence the legislator's judgment. . . .

Corruption as the distortion of influence sees the legislator as properly attentive to the desires and preferences of those he represents. In a well-functioning democracy, the legislator responds to these desires and preferences. [On this view,] corruption occurs when a legislator weighs the preferences of some too heavily, especially when the legislator considers the wishes of wealthy contributors more than others. . . .

A third view of proper legislative conduct [requires] only that the legislator not actually exchange votes or favors for money. [Corruption], on this view, is narrowly defined as quid pro quo corruption—that is, the sale of some public favor. . . .

[W]hen the Court defines corruption [in its campaign finance case law], it inescapably puts forward a conception of the proper role of a legislator in a democracy. That is a task that the Court should be cautious to take up. [Because there] are many reasonable ways to instantiate representative democracy, [we] should eschew judicial actions that adopt one view of representative democracy [over another]. Because judicial pronouncements about what constitutes corruption entail commitments to contested conceptions of democracy, there are strong reasons for courts to avoid defining corruption."

b. R. Post, Citizens Divided: Campaign Finance Reform and the Constitution 4, 60-65 (2014):

"[P]roponents of campaign finance reform have failed to advance justifications for regulation that can be inoculated with basic First Amendment principles. They have instead promoted justifications like 'distortion' or 'equality,' which are inconsistent with essential premises of First Amendment doctrine. . . .

[F]irst Amendment rights presuppose that elections must be structured to select for persons who possess the "communion of interests and sympathy of sentiments" to remain responsive to public opinion. [The concept of "electoral integrity" denominates] elections that have the property of choosing candidates whom the people trust to possess this sympathy and connection. Without electoral integrity, First Amendment rights necessarily fail to achieve their constitutional purpose. If the people do not believe that elected officials listen to public opinion, participation in public discourse, no matter how free, cannot create the experience of self-government. . . .

The democratic structure and legitimacy of our government depend on electoral integrity. Yet the Court in its campaign finance opinions has not considered the state's interest in promoting the electoral integrity required by the First Amendment. The Court has instead been preoccupied by the attempt to balance First Amendment rights against the need to prevent [quid pro quo] corruption. . . .

If [we] reformulate our campaign finance jurisprudence upon the principle of electoral integrity, [we] may create a more enduring foundation for the contested area of campaign finance reform. [This] formulation of the issue [requires] us merely to affirm [that] Americans cannot maintain the blessings of self-government unless they believe that elections produce representatives who are responsive to public opinion. [Electoral] integrity is a compelling government interest because without it Americans have no reason to exercise the communicative rights guaranteed by the First Amendment.

[There] are good reasons to worry that electoral integrity is today under threat. Americans' trust and confidence in their representative institutions has fallen to record lows; we are [experiencing] what most regard as a crisis of representation. In such circumstances it is especially disappointing that the Court seems unwilling to recognize even the existence of the constitutional principle of electoral integrity. . . ."

 c. Lessig, What an Originalist Would Understand "Corruption" to Mean, 102 Cal. L. Rev. 1, 3-11 (2014):

"The United States [effectively] has two distinct elections. One election is discrete—call it the "voting election." [All] "voters" are permitted to participate in that election. [The] other election is continuous—call it the "money election." It happens throughout the election cycle. Any citizen [is] permitted to participate in that money election. [To] be allowed to run in the voting election [one] has to do extremely well in the money election. [In] the 2012 election cycle, 84 percent of the House candidates and 67 percent of the Senate candidates with more

VII. Freedom of Expression

money than their opponents won. [The] money election produces a subtle, perhaps camouflaged bending [of the process] to keep the funders of the money election happy. [Importantly,] the relevant number of funders is [small]. [In] the 2012 presidential election 0.000032 percent [of Americans]—or 99 Americans—provided 60 percent of the individual Super PAC money spent. . . .

[The] way we fund elections has created a dependency that conflicts with the dependency intended by the Constitution. That conflict is a corruption. [In] the Framers' language, [the concept of "corruption"] included a collective sense—the corruption of an institution, or a people, and not just a person. [Congress] was intended to be "dependent on the people alone." It has become dependent upon an additional dependence, "the funders" of campaigns. Because of who "the funders" are, this additional dependence is a conflicting dependence, and that conflict constitutes "corruption."

This sense of corruption, as constituted by "improper dependence," was perfectly familiar to the Framers. It is with this sense of "corruption" in mind that we can see why our current Congress is "corrupt." For the Framers, Congress was [to] have an intended dependence. That dependence was to be, as James Madison wrote in The Federalist No. 52, "on the people." [For the Framers,] the anti-corruption challenge was not how to ensure that criminals stayed away from Congress; the challenge was how to secure the influences most likely to align the institution to its proper ends by protecting it from improper dependence. [It] is this fact that makes the current Supreme Court's jurisprudence about "corruption" so weird. [Only] a non-originalist could embrace [the Court's] position."

d. L. Tribe & J. Matz, Uncertain Justice: The Roberts Court and the Constitution 100-101, 104-105, 108-109, 112-113 (2014):

"*Citizens United* decisively rejected the anti-distortion justification for campaign finance laws. . . . To be sure, money can powerfully advantage a speaker in the marketplace of ideas [and] concentrated wealth, left unregulated, can create a risk that most headlines and TV ads will be controlled by a small group. . . . Still, it would be a mistake to leave judgments about the "proper" distribution of speech to politicians. Arming them with a roving license to level the playing field by silencing or adjusting the volume of disfavored speakers is an invitation to self-serving behavior and, ultimately, tyranny. The anti-distortion argument can too easily lead down this dangerous path, and [the Court] rightly discarded it. . . .

[Another argument made against the Court's approach in these cases focuses on a broad conception of "corruption."] "Corruption," in this view, occurs when politicians become dependent on a wealthy clique and government is no longer responsive to the public interest. [The justices in the majority in these cases] are unreservedly hostile to such arguments. They worry that noble-sounding rationales for campaign finance laws can too easily conceal efforts by incumbents to protect themselves and punish their enemies. [The Court has not adopted] a narrow definition of corruption because it is naïve or apathetic. It has done so because it doubts that the Court [can] create workable First Amendment law that adequately guards against abuse by politicians. Embracing a broader view of the anti-corruption interest risked creating an exception that swallowed the rule. . . .

In an age of political dysfunction, the extraordinary sums of money that candidates avidly pursue present hard questions about how to reconcile competing national values. [The Court's decisions in these cases will likely affect] policy outcomes by causing an across-the-board realignment of government priorities toward interests backed by big money. Every capable politician has an eye on the next election and a keen sense of who provided support last time, who didn't, who might be persuaded to shift their opinions, and how that might be achieved. [The Court's decisions are] therefore likely to trigger a self-reinforcing cycle. [As] the group of victorious candidates comes to consist mainly of politicians who can successfully navigate these structures and depend on them for reelection, the impetus for change among officeholders will fade. [Perhaps the best solution would be the enactment of new disclosure requirements.] In the post-*Citizens United* era, transparency would provide at least a measure of reassurance. . . ."

e. In Six Amendments: How and Why We Should Change the Constitution (2014), former Justice John Paul Stevens proposed the following amendment to the Constitution:

> Neither the First Amendment nor any other provision of this Constitution shall be construed to prohibit the Congress or any state from imposing reasonable limits on the amount of money that candidates for public office, or their supporters, may spend in election campaigns.

Page 1404. Before section 3 of the Note, add the following:

Lane v. Franks, 134 S. Ct. 2369 (2014) (public employee who testifies under subpoena about a matter related to his public employment is protected by the First Amendment, despite *Garcetti*, where his testimony was not required by "his ordinary job responsibilities").

Page 1418. After section 5 of the Note, add the following:

5a. *Conditions on recipients of public funds.* See Agency for International Development v. Alliance for Open Society International, 133 S. Ct. 2321 (2013), insert in this Supplement for page 1337 of the main volume.

VII. Freedom of Expression

Page 1418. At the end of section 6 of the Note, add the following:

In Harris v. Quinn, 134 S. Ct. 2618 (2014), the Court considered the constitutionality of an Illinois law that allowed Medicaid recipients who normally would need institutional care to hire a "personal assistant" (PA) to provide homecare services. Under the law, the Medicaid homecare recipients and the state both play a role in the employment relationship with the PAs.

Pursuant to this program, the Service Employees International Union (SEIU) was designated the exclusive union representative for the PAs. SEIU entered into collective-bargaining agreements with the state that included an agency-fee provision, which requires PAs who do not wish to join the union to pay the union a fee for the cost of collective-bargaining expenses, but not for the cost of any political activities of the union unrelated to collective bargaining. A group of PAs who had not joined the union and did not want to pay *any* union fees brought this suit claiming that the law violated their First Amendment right not to be compelled to support the union. Pursuant to *Abood*, the lower courts rejected this challenge and upheld the law.

In a five-to-four decision, the Supreme Court reversed. In an opinion by Justice Alito, the Court cast serious doubt on *Abood*, insofar as it permitted the state to compel non-union members to pay union fees even for the costs of collective-bargaining activities that benefit them. Ultimately, though, the Court invalidated the law without overruling *Abood*, by distinguishing the specific factual situation in the context of PAs from the situations in other public union arrangements. Justice Kagan, joined by Justices Ginsburg, Breyer, and Sotomayor, dissented. Kagan insisted that *Abood* reflected sound First Amendment principles and that the situation in this case was not in any principled way distinguishable from the Court's prior decisions.

F. *Freedom of the Press*

Page 1426. After section 2 of the Note, add the following:

2a. *Protecting the anonymity of the source*. Instead of focusing on the First Amendment right of the reporter to keep sources confidential, would it make more sense to focus on the First Amendment right of the source to engage in anonymous speech? After all, in a series of decisions, including *Talley v. California, McIntyre v. Ohio Elections Commission, NAACP v. Alabama,* and *Brown v. Socialist Workers*, the Court has protected a right to anonymous speech, noting that anonymous speech has "played an important role in the progress of mankind" and that "persecuted groups" throughout history "have been able to criticize oppressive practices either anonymously or not at all." Consider Jones, Re-Thinking Reporter's Privilege, 111 Mich. L. Rev. 1221 (2013):

> A confidential source who does not wish to have her name revealed is analytically indistinguishable from any other author, writer, or speaker who wishes to convey information anonymously. Like the leafleteer in *Talley* ... and the concerned taxpayer in *McIntyre*, ... a confidential source offers information that she wishes to make public without attribution ... for any number of reasons that the Court has acknowledged as valid. [The] source should be entitled to protection under the anonymous speech doctrine for statements made to a reporter in confidence.

2b. *Investigative journalism or criminal solicitation?* Suppose a reporter persuades a public employee unlawfully to leak classified information. Can the reporter constitutionally be convicted of the crime of criminal solicitation? Recall *O'Brien*. Suppose a journalist conducts an illegal wiretap in order to prove that a congressman took a bribe. Would her conduct be protected by the First Amendment? If not, is criminal solicitation any different? See G. Stone, Top Secret: When Government Keeps Us in the Dark 29-38 (2007) (arguing that because prosecution of journalists for the crime of solicitation would interject "government into the very heart of the journalist-source relationship" and thus "have a serious chilling effect" on legitimate and important journalist-source exchanges, the government should not be able to punish journalists for encouraging public employees to disclose classified information unless the journalist (a) expressly incites the leak and (b) knows that publication of the information would likely cause imminent and grave harm to the national security). Can that position be reconciled with the wiretap example or with *Branzburg*?

VIII
THE CONSTITUTION AND RELIGION

A. Introduction: Historical and Analytical Overview

Page 1467. At the end of section 9 of the Note, add the following:

For recent discussions of this question, see Leiter, Why Tolerate Religion? (2012), offering a perspective from moral and political theory, and Koppelman, Defending American Religious Neutrality (2013), offering a perspective from political theory and law. See also Schwartzman, What If Religion Is Not Special?, 79 U. Chi. L. Rev. 1351 (2012):

> [Many] of the most widely held normative justifications for favoring (or disfavoring) religion are prone to predictable forms of internal incoherence [and] accounts [that] manage to avoid such incoherence succeed only at the cost of committing other serious errors, especially in allowing various types of unfairness toward religious believers, nonbelievers, or both. The upshot of all this is that principles of disestablishment and free exercise ought to be conceived in terms that go beyond the category of religion. Instead of disabling or protecting only religious beliefs and practices, the law ought to provide similar treatment for comparable secular ethical, moral, and philosophical views.

B. The Establishment Clause

Page 1494. At the end of note 6, add the following:

6a. *Marsh revisited or extended?* Town of Greece v. Galloway, 134 S. Ct. 1811 (2014), involved the prayer practices of the town board of Greece, a suburb of Rochester, New York. Starting in 1999, the board opened its meetings with, among other matters, a prayer given by guest chaplains chosen from a list of congregations in the town directory, nearly all of which are Christian. Some of the ministers "spoke in a distinctly Christian idiom," including invoking "the saving sacrifice of Jesus Christ on the cross."

Justice Kennedy wrote an opinion that was in part for the Court, and in part only for himself and Chief Justice Roberts and Justice Alito. The Court upheld the town's practices. It relied heavily on *Marsh*, which "[must] not be understood as permitting a practice that would amount to a constitutional violation if not for its historical foundation. The case teaches instead that the Establishment Clause must be interpreted 'by reference to historical practices and understandings.' [The] Court's inquiry [must] be to determine whether the prayer practice in the town of Greece fits within the tradition long followed in Congress and the state legislatures." But "[an] insistence on nonsectarian or ecumenical prayer as a single, fixed, standard is not consistent with the tradition of legislative [prayer]. [To] hold that invocations must be nonsectarian would force the legislatures [and] the courts [to] act as supervisors and censors of religious speech, [which] would involve government in religious matters to a far greater degree [than] is the case under the town's current practice." Justice Kennedy also wrote, "If the course and practice over time shows that the invocations denigrate nonbelievers or religious minorities, threaten damnation, or preach conversion, many present may consider the prayer to fall short of the desire to elevate the purpose of the occasion and to unite lawmakers in their common effort. That circumstance would present a different [case]." Noting that "two remarks" by guest chaplains "strayed from the rationale set out in *Marsh*," he wrote that "they do not despoil a practice that on the whole reflects and embraces our tradition. Absent a pattern of prayers that over time denigrate, proselytize, or betray an impermissible government purpose, a challenge based solely on the content of a prayer will not likely establish a constitutional violation." The town's efforts to locate guest chaplains were "reasonable," and did "not reflect an aversion or bias on the part of town leaders against minority faiths. So long as the town maintains a policy of nondiscrimination, the Constitution does not require it to search beyond its borders for non-Christian prayer givers in an effort to achieve religious balancing."

In the part of the opinion joined only by the Chief Justice and Justice Alito, Justice Kennedy addressed and rejected the argument that the prayer practice coerced participation. As to coercion, "The inquiry remains a fact-sensitive one that considers both the setting in which the prayer arises and the audience to whom it is directed," again "valuated against the backdrop of historical practice." "It is presumed that the reasonable observer is acquainted with this tradition and understands that its purposes are to lend gravity to public proceedings and to acknowledge the place religion holds in the lives of many private citizens, not to afford government an opportunity to proselytize or force truant constituents into the pews. That many appreciate these acknowledgments of the divine in our public institutions does not suggest that those who disagree are compelled to join the expression or approve its content." But "[t]he analysis would be different if town board members directed the public to participate in the prayers, singled out dissidents for opprobrium, or indicated that their decisions might be influenced by a person's acquiescence in the prayer opportunity." Addressing the respondents' claim that "the prayers gave them offense and made them feel excluded and disrespected," Justice Kennedy wrote, "Offense [does] not equate to coercion."

Justice Thomas, joined in part by Justice Scalia, wrote separately. Justice Thomas repeated his argument that the Establishment Clause was not made applicable to the states by the Fourteenth Amendment. In addition, he argued that "the municipal prayers [bear] no resemblance to the coercive state establishments that existed at the founding." The coercion relevant to Establishment Clause analysis "is actual legal coercion, [not] the 'subtle coercive pressures' allegedly felt by [respondents]."

Justice Kagan, joined by Justices Ginsburg, Breyer, and Sotomayor, dissented. Justice Breyer also dissented in a separate opinion. For Justice Kagan, "[t]he practice [here] differs from the one sustained in [*Marsh*] because Greece's town meetings involve participation by ordinary citizens, and the invocations given—directly to those citizens—were predominantly sectarian. [Greece's] Board did nothing to recognize religious diversity. [The] Town never sought (except briefly when this suit was filed) to involve, accommodate, or in any way reach out to adherents of non-Christian religions." She agreed that "Greece's Board [has] legislative functions," but its "meetings are also occasions for ordinary citizens to engage with and petition their government, often on highly individualized matters. That feature calls for Board members to exercise special care to ensure that the prayers offered [respect] each and every member of the community as an equal citizen." The sessions in *Marsh* at which prayers were offered were "floor sessions [for] elected lawyers. Members of the public take no part. [Greece's] town meetings [revolve] around ordinary members of the community," who "urge [changes] in the Board's policies [and] then, in which are essentially adjudicatory hearings, they request the Board to grant [applications] for various permits."

> Let's say that a Muslim citizen of Greece goes before the Board to [request] some permit. [Just] before she gets to speak her piece, a minister deputized by the Town asks her to pray "in the name of God's only son Jesus Christ." She must think [that] Christian worship has become entwined with local governance. And now she faces a choice—to pray alongside the majority [or] somehow to register her deeply felt difference. [That] is no easy call—especially given that the room is small and her every action [will] be noticed. She does not wish to be rude to her neighbors, nor does she wish

to aggravate the Board members whom she will soon be trying to persuade. And yet she does not want to acknowledge Christ's divinity. [So] assume she declines to participate with the others in the first act of the meeting—or even [stands] up and leaves the room. [She] becomes a different kind of citizen. [And] she thus stands at a remove, based solely on religion, from her fellow citizens and her elected representatives. Everything about that situation [infringes] the First Amendment.

Justice Kagan would allow some prayer activities. "What the circumstances here demand is the recognition that we are a pluralistic people. [If] the Town Board had let its chaplains know that they should speak in nonsectarian terms, [then] no one would have valid grounds for complaint. [Or] it might have invited clergy of many faiths to serve as chaplains. [But] Greece could not do what it did: infuse a participatory government body with one (and only one) faith." For her, "[when] a citizen stands before her government, [her] religious beliefs do not enter into the picture. The government she faces favors no particular religion, either by word or by deed. And that government [imposes] no religious tests on its citizens, sorts none of them by faith, and permits no exclusion based on belief. When a person goes to court, a polling place, or an immigration proceeding, [government] officials do not engage in sectarian worship, nor do they ask her to do likewise. They all participate in the business of government not as Christians, Jews, Muslims (and more), but only as Americans—none of them different from any other for that civic purpose."

Justice Alito, joined by Justice Scalia, responded to Justice Kagan in a concurring opinion, calling "the narrow aspect" of her dissent's objections to the holding "really quite niggling." He argued that "there [is] no historical support for the proposition that only generic prayer is allowed," and observed that "as our country has become more diverse, composing a prayer that is acceptable to all members of the community who hold religious beliefs has become [harder.]" Further, "if a town attempts to go beyond simply recommending that a guest chaplain deliver a prayer that is broadly acceptable, [the] town will [encounter] sensitive problems," including possible prescreening or reviewing prayers. The alternative of compiling a list of clergy from numerous traditions to serve as guest chaplains meant that Justice Kagan's objection was only the "[the] town's clerical employees did a bad job in compiling the list" they used.

Page 1499. At the end of section 2 of the Note, add the following:

Consider these observations, from Koppelman, The New American Civil Religion: Lessons for Italy, Geo. Wash. Int'l L. Rev. 961, 866 (2010):

Douglas Laycock thinks that a lesson [is] that "separationist groups should sue immediately when they encounter any religious practice newly sponsored by the government." That is precisely the right lesson. [New] sponsorship of religious practices is far more likely to represent a contemporaneous effort to intervene in a live religious controversy than the perpetuation of old forms.

D. *Permissible Accommodation*

Page 1549. At the end of note 5, add the following:

The Religious Freedom Restoration Act was held unconstitutional with respect to state legislation, but remains applicable to federal legislation. See Gonzales v. O Centro Espirita Beneficente Uniao do Vegetal, 546 U.S. 418 (2006). For a controversial application of the Act, see Burwell v. Hobby Lobby Stores, Inc., ___ S. Ct. ___ (2014) (rejecting the argument that, with respect to those entitled to raise RFRA claims, the statute "did no more than codify this Court's pre-*Smith* precedents" and holding that a closely held, for-profit corporation with religious objections to certain forms of birth control was entitled to a statutory exemption from a requirement that any insurance policy it provided to its workers cover contraception).

IX
STATE ACTION, BASELINES, AND THE PROBLEM OF PRIVATE POWER

A. State Action, Federalism, and Individual Autonomy

Page 1561. At the end of the Note, add the following:

Is there an "individual action" doctrine that complements the state action requirement? Recall that in National Federation of Independent Business v. Sebelius, 132 S. Ct. 2566 (2012), the Supreme Court held that the "individual mandate" of the Affordable Care Act, which required certain individuals to acquire insurance in private markets, exceeded Congress's power under the commerce clause. (Sebelius is discussed at page 218 of the main volume.) Consider Note, NFIB v. Sebelius and the Individualization of the State Action Doctrine, 127 Harv. L. Rev. 1174, 1174-1175 (2014):

> [*Sebelius's*] distinction between activity and inactivity [mirrors] [the] state action doctrine. . . .
> Both the state action and the individual action doctrines share an analogous analytic framework, and they serve analogous functions. The doctrines police a boundary between the citizen and the state by limiting federal power to contexts either in which the state has acted or in which individuals have acted. In doing so the doctrines construct a realm of individual autonomy free from certain types of governmental intrusions. [*Sebelius*] transposes and grafts onto the Commerce Clause many of the same commitments that drive

the Court's state action jurisprudence, including limitations on the manner in which Congress can regulate nominally private decisionmaking.

E. *Unconstitutional Conditions and the Benefit/Burden Distinction*

Page 1613. At the bottom of the page, add the following:

The Court elaborated on its *Nollan* holding in Koontz v. St. Johns River Water Management District, 570 U.S. 133 S. Ct. 2586 (2013), where it held that the same principle was applicable when, instead of accepting the condition, as the landowner had in *Nollan,* the landholder rejected the condition leading to the denial of a permit. Writing for five justices, Justice Alito stated:

> Our decisions [reflect] two realities of the permitting process. The first is that land-use permit applicants are especially vulnerable to the type of coercion that the unconstitutional conditions doctrine prohibits because the government often has broad discretion to deny a permit that is worth far more than property it would like to take. By conditioning a building permit on the owner's deeding over a public right-of-way, for example, the government can pressure an owner into voluntarily giving up property for which the Fifth Amendment would otherwise require just compensation. So long as the building permit is more valuable than any just compensation the owner could hope to receive for the right-of-way, the owner is likely to accede to the government's demand no matter how unreasonable. Extortionate demands of this sort frustrate the Fifth Amendment right to just compensation, and the unconstitutional conditions doctrine prohibits them.
>
> The second reality of the permitting process is that many proposed land uses threaten to impose costs on the public that dedications of property can offset. [Insisting] that landowners internalize the negative externalities of their conduct is a hallmark of responsible land-use policy, and we have long sustained such regulations against constitutional attack.
>
> *Nollan* [accommodates] both realities by allowing the government to condition approval of a permit on the dedication of property to the public so long as there is a "nexus" and "rough proportionality" between the property the government demands and the social costs of the applicant's proposal. Our precedents thus enable permitting authorities to insist that applicants

bear the full costs of their proposals while still forbidding the government from engaging in "out-and-out . . . extortion" that would thwart the Fifth Amendment right to just compensation.

Page 1620. At the end of the Note, add the following:

(f) For an interesting unconstitutional conditions decision, see Agency for International Development v. Alliance for Open Society International, 133 S. Ct. 2321 (2013). By statute, Congress authorized the appropriation of billions of dollars to fund efforts by nongovernmental organizations to combat HIV/AIDS worldwide. Congress also imposed two conditions on the receipt of funds: (1) no funds "may be used to promote or advocate the legalization or practice of prostitution"; and (2) no funds may be used by an organization "that does not have a policy explicitly opposing prostitution."

The Court struck down the second condition. It emphasized a distinction between two kinds of conditions: (1) those that define the limits of the Government spending program (specifying the activities Congress wants to subsidize) and (2) those that seek to leverage funding to regulate speech outside the contours of the federal program itself. While Congress may limit its own spending, so that cases that fall within category (1) are permissible, Congress faces constitutional limits when it restricts speech in category (2).

The Court held that the restriction at issue fell in the second category: "By demanding that funding recipients adopt—as their own—the Government's view on an issue of public concern, the condition by its very nature affects 'protected conduct outside the scope of the federally funded program.' By requiring recipients to profess a specific belief, the [requirement] goes beyond defining the limits of the federally funded program to defining the recipient." In the Court's view, the requirement "goes beyond preventing recipients from using private funds in a way that would undermine the federal program. It requires them to pledge allegiance to the Government's policy of eradicating prostitution."

Justice Scalia, joined by Justice Thomas, dissented. He contended that the requirement at issue "is nothing more than a means of selecting suitable agents to implement the Government's chosen strategy to eradicate HIV/AIDS. That is perfectly permissible under the Constitution." In his view, "the government may enlist the assistance of those who believe in its ideas to carry them to fruition; and it need not enlist for that purpose those who oppose or do not support the ideas. That seems to me a matter of the most common common sense. For example: One of the purposes of America's foreign-aid programs is the fostering of goodwill towards this country. If the organization Hamas—reputed to have an efficient system for delivering welfare—were excluded from a program for the distribution of U.S. food assistance, no one could reasonably object. And that would remain true if Hamas were an organization of United States citizens entitled to the protection of the Constitution. [And] the same is true when the rejected organization is not affirmatively opposed to, but merely unsupportive of, the object of the federal program, which appears to be the case here. (Respondents do not promote prostitution, but neither do they wish to oppose it.) A federal program to encourage healthy eating habits need not be administered by the American Gourmet Society, which has nothing against healthy food but does not insist upon it."